C I T Y P A C K
Venice

By Tim Jepson

Fodor's

Fodor's Travel Publications, Inc.
New York • Toronto • London • Sydney • Auckland

HTTP://WWW.FODORS.COM/

Contents

About this book...4

About this book

KEY TO SYMBOLS

✚ map reference on the fold-out map accompanying this book (see below)

✉ address

☎ telephone number

◷ opening times

🍽 restaurant or café on premises or nearby

Ⓜ nearest Metro (subway) train station

🚉 nearest overground train station

🚌 nearest bus route

⛴ nearest riverboat or ferry stop

♿ facilities for visitors with disabilities

✋ admission charge

↔ other nearby places of interest

❓ tours, lectures, or special events

▶ indicates the page where you will find a fuller description

ℹ tourist information

Citypack Venice is divided into six sections to cover the six most important aspects of your visit to Venice. It includes:

- The author's view of the city and its people
- Itineraries, walks, and excursions
- The top 25 sights to visit—as selected by the author
- Features about different aspects of the city that make it special
- Detailed listings of hotels, restaurants, stores, and nightlife
- Practical information

In addition, easy-to-read side panels provide fascinating extra facts and snippets, highlights of places to visit and invaluable practical advice.

CROSS-REFERENCES

To help you make the most of your visit, cross-references, indicated by ▶ , show you where to find additional information about a place or subject.

MAPS

- **The fold-out map** in the wallet at the back of the book is a comprehensive street map of Venice. All the map references given in the book refer to this map. For example, the Palazzo Ducale on Piazzetta San Marco has the following information: ✚ H12—indicating the grid square of the map in which the Palazzo Ducale will be found.
- **The downtown maps** found on the inside front and back covers of the book itself are for quick reference. They show the Top 25 Sights, described on pages 24–48, which are clearly plotted by number (❶ – ㉕, not page number) from west to east.

PRICES

Where appropriate, an indication of the cost of an establishment is given by **$** signs: **$$$** denotes higher prices, **$$** denotes average prices, while **$** denotes lower charges.

VENICE *life*

INTRODUCING VENICE

Venice has been seducing visitors for centuries, its impossible watery setting and fairytale appearance casting a spell whose potency remains undimmed by mass tourism. More than most cities Venice repays those who make a lingering acquaintance and who show a willingness to leave the main sights in favor of the evocative quiet squares and small churches.

Orientation The city sits at the heart of a lagoon, separated from the open sea by a line of defensive sand bars. Its 118 islands, 400-plus bridges and 170 canals are divided into six districts, or *sestieri*. Half of these (San Polo, Dorsoduro, and Santa Croce) lie west of the Grand Canal and half to the east (San Marco, Castello, and Cannaregio). The city may seem labyrinthine, but in practice the web of streets is easier to navigate than it first appears.

Planning itineraries Once you have grasped the city's layout, the best way to see individual attractions is in self-contained clusters. Study the map to locate the top 25 sights and ascertain which other more minor sights lie close by. Bear in mind that only three bridges cross the Grand Canal, so plan itineraries carefully to avoid

The Future

Venice is no longer sinking, contrary to popular belief. Water was once extracted for industrial use on the mainland, causing the clay and silt underpinning Venice to contract and shrink, and Venice to sink. However, when this practise was curtailed in the 1970s the sinking stopped, though the city did not recover the height lost. Instead it is threatened today by pollution from Marghera and Mestre, two industrial towns on the mainland. Damp and salt combine with sulfur dioxide emissions to produce a corrosive brew that is lethal to stonework. Dredging and land reclamation have exacerbated the risk of flooding, a danger many do not believe will be removed by the system of steel dikes (known as MOSE) currently being built across the lagoon. Equally damaging to Venice's long-term future is the city's dwindling population; many "Venetians" now commute to the city from Mestre or Marghera. Schemes to preserve Venice for Venetians—modern houses, jobs, a new metro— are often at odds with those aimed at preserving the city for posterity.

Looking from the Piazzetta toward Salute

unnecessary walking. Also learn to use the *traghetti* (ferries) that cross the Canal at strategic points, and do not overlook the *vaporetti* (water buses) as a means of sightseeing, particularly the No. 1, which lumbers along the Grand Canal.

When time is short It is best to see anything on your first morning *apart* from Piazza San Marco, the Doge's Palace or the Basilica di San Marco. Start instead with something more modest so that the crowds do not turn you against the city on your first acquaintance.

Once you have a feel for the city's intimate side you can move to the bigger draws: to the two key galleries, the Accademia and Collezione Peggy Guggenheim; to the two major churches, SS Giovanni e Paolo and Santa Maria Gloriosa dei Frari; to the two best museums, the Correr and Ca' d'Oro; and to the finest *scuole* (religious and charitable institutions), the Scuola Grande di San Rocco and Scuola di San Giorgio degli Schiavoni. Thereafter, you can decide between more museums or smaller churches. Finally, you can brace yourself for the "big two": the Palazzo Ducale (Doge's Palace) and Basilica di San Marco (St. Mark's).

Discoveries

Venice's best moments often occur away from the main sights. Thus you should take a boat along the Grand Canal just for the ride (▶ 24), or you should visit the Rialto markets at the crack of dawn before the crowds arrive (▶ 81). Alternatively, an ice cream or *cappuccino* in a square is ideal if you wish to experience the city's quieter side (▶ 54–55 and 74–75). There is little that can beat an aerial view of the city, preferably from the top of the San Giorgio Maggiore (▶ 56), and no other city offers more surprises for those who are prepared to walk and wander its streets at random (▶ 16–18).

VENICE PEOPLE

Enjoying the sun

Character

"Like the tide—six hours up and six hours down" is how one proverb summarizes the Venetians' reputed tendency toward swings of character and mercurial moods. They are also reputed to be sardonic, and to feel the separateness, wistfulness and "introspective melancholy" of an island race. Past history and isolation have also given rise to an un-Italian instinct for cooperation and sense of civic pride. Venetians are also polite and reserved, even in the face of their city's invasion by tourists. Other Italians consider them wily, cunning, and clever in speech. They are also considered by Italians to be lazy (wrongly), and are said to enjoy their wine more than they should...

Many Venetians start their day on a boat or train. Some commute from the mainland, leaving their cars in the vast parking lots at the end of Venice's only "road"—the causeway that crosses the lagoon from Mestre (officially a part of "Venice"). Others board the water buses (*vaporetti*) that ply the city's canals, heading to work, school, or university in a city where even the traffic jams are beautiful. Breakfast for most is a hurried *espresso* and *brioche* at one of the city's many small bars.

Mid-morning sees many Venetian mothers at large, either shopping in the Rialto markets or chatting to friends as their children play in the city's palace-lined squares. This is also the time when a veritable army of elderly women hits the streets to walk their dogs. Lunchtime sees another rush hour on the water as people return home for lunch, battling with tourists for a place on the laden *vaporetti*. Some head for Venice's traditional *enoteche*, where a glass of wine and light meal take the place of the traditional long lunch.

In the dog days of summer the afternoons pass slowly as the Venetians wisely keep to their houses to escape the heat of the sun. Those not so lucky might instead take an *ombra*, or "shadow", the name given to the Venetian habit of breaking off work for a glass of wine in one of the cave-like *bacari* (wine bars) that cluster in certain parts of the city. Later on, people might sip an aperitif or Prosecco, a local sparkling wine, before heading home.

Evenings are sedate, most Venetians preferring a meal at home with friends or a quiet drink to a meal out or a night on the tiles. Venice has little nightlife, so for entertainment many locals head for Mestre. Others content themselves with dinner, preferably in a restaurant undiscovered by tourists, or a stroll followed by an ice cream (*gelato*) or digestif (after-diner liqueur) in one of the city's café-ringed piazzas.

VENICE IN FIGURES

GEOGRAPHY
- Latitude: 41°N
- Longitude: 12°E
- Height above sea level: 32 in.
- Height of 1966 floods: 6ft.
- Highest point: Campanile (323ft.)
- Average January temperature: 39°F
- Average July temperature: 75°F
- Average January rainfall: 2.2 in.
- Average July rainfall: 1.4 in.

PEOPLE
- Population after 1630 plague: 102,000
- Population in 1938: 164,000
- Population in 1994: 72,000
- Population under 10 in 1994: 4,530
- Population over 60 in 1994: 23,300
- Average age in 1994: 44
- Population of Mestre in 1938: 65,000
- Population of Mestre in 1990: 192,000
- People leaving Venice annually: 1,500
- Cost of living: 1 percent higher than Milan and 3 percent higher than Rome
- Percentage of work force involved in tourism: over 50 percent
- Number of souvenir shops: around 450
- Number of plumbers: 13

CITY
- Official age in 2000: 1,579 years
- Distance from west to east: 3 miles
- Distance from north to south: 1.2 miles
- Size equivalent to: New York's Central Park
- Number of alleys (estimate): 3,000
- Length of alleys if laid end to end: 120 miles
- Number of street cats in 1994: 2,327
- Number of bridges (estimate): 400
- Number of islands: 118
- Number of canals: 170
- Rate of sinking: 0 in. a year
- Year sinking stopped: 1983
- Visitors per year (estimate): 12,000,000
- Most visitors in one day (estimate): 150,000 (on July 15, 1989)
- Number of homes without bathrooms: 2,000
- Amount of sulfur dioxide gas produced by Marghera's factories: 55,000 tons per year
- Buildings on Grand Canal with foundations in need of repair: 60 percent

9

A Chronology

800 BC	Sporadic settlement of the lagoon by the Venetii and Euganei tribes.
250 BC	Rome conquers northeastern Italy (*Venetia*) and founds important colonies at Padua, Verona, Altinium, and Aquileia.
AD 375	The first Barbarian invasions threaten the Roman Empire.
402	Alaric the Goth sacks Altinium and other north-eastern colonies. A vision of the Virgin guides refugees to an island in the lagoon.
421	According to legend Venice is founded on March 25, the Feast Day of the Virgin Mary.
453	Aquileia is sacked by Attila the Hun, prompting another exodus of refugees to the lagoon.
466	The lagoon's settlements elect "maritime tribunes" to coordinate policy.
697	Paoluccio Anafesto, traditional first doge ("leader"), is elected.
726	The first documented doge, Orso Ipato, rules the lagoon from the now-vanished colony of Heraclea.
810	Lagoon dwellers gather on the more easily defended islands of the Rivus Altus (Rialto).
814	Work begins on the Doge's Palace.
828	Venetian merchants steal the relics of St. Mark from Alexandria.
829	Work begins on the Basilica di San Marco
1000	The Marriage to the Sea ceremony is inaugurated to celebrate Doge Pietro Orseolo II's defeat of Dalmatian pirates in the Adriatic.
1099	Venice provides ships for the First Crusade.
1171	Venice's six districts, or *sestieri*, are founded.

1173	Work begins on the first Rialto bridge.
1204	Venice sacks Constantinople and acquires much of the former Byzantine Empire.
1269	Marco Polo leaves Venice to travel in the East.
1309	Work begins on the present Doge's Palace.
1348	The Black Death kills half the population.
1380	Victory over the Genoese wins Venice naval supremacy in the Adriatic and Mediterranean.
1406	Venice defeats Padua and Verona to lay the foundations of a mainland empire.
1453	Venice's power is at its height, but the Turks take Constantinople.
1498	Vasco da Gama's discovery of the Cape route to the East weakens Venice's trading monopolies.
1571	Venice loses Cyprus to the Turks.
1669	The Turks take Crete from the Venetians.
1718	The loss of Morea marks the end of Venice's maritime empire.
1797	Napoleon invades Italy: the last doge abdicates and the Venetian Republic comes to an end.
1814	After Napoleon's defeat, the Congress of Vienna cedes Venice and the Veneto to Austria.
1848	Daniele Manin leads an unsuccessful Venetian uprising against Austrian rule.
1866	Venice joins a united Italy.
1902	The Campanile in Piazza San Marco collapses.
1966	Devastating floods ravage Venice.
1988	Works begins on the lagoon's flood barrier.

PEOPLE & EVENTS FROM HISTORY

Antonio Vivaldi

Vivaldi was born in Venice in 1678, the son of a violinist. Although ordained as a priest, he devoted much of his life to music, teaching the violin at La Pietà, an

orphanage whose girls received a musical training as part of their state-funded education (in time such orphanages became renowned as centers of musical excellence). La Pietà's resident orchestra enabled him to create a wealth of musical compositions, including 50 operas and 454 concertos, as well as the famous "Four Seasons." Although praised at the height of his career, his star soon waned, and in 1740 he was forced to leave Venice for Vienna to seek work. He died a year later and received only a pauper's funeral.

CASANOVA

Casanova was born in Venice in 1725. Although destined for the priesthood, his adolescent follies caused him to be expelled from his seminary. He was then exiled from Venice for five years, during which time he traveled between Paris, Dresden, Prague, and Vienna. On his return in 1755 he was imprisoned on charges of sorcery. In 1756, after 15 months in the Palazzo Ducale's prisons, he made a daring escape to France, where he introduced Paris to the lottery before being forced to flee from angry creditors. He then visited London, Berlin, St. Petersburg, and Warsaw, but was forced to leave the last after a duel. After a period in Spain he returned to Venice, where he became a spy for the Inquisition. A libel suit forced his departure from the city, and he spent his remaining years as a librarian for a Bohemian count.

MARCO POLO

Marco Polo was born in Venice around 1254, the son of a merchant adventurer. In 1269 he joined his father on a journey that would last over 20 years. He traveled through present-day Turkey and Palestine, crossed the deserts of eastern Iran and Afghanistan, and in 1275 arrived at the court of Kublai Khan. Over the next 17 years he served the Mongol emperor, traversing China and the Far East on a series of diplomatic and trade missions. In 1292 he decided to head for home, travelling to Venice by way of Vietnam, Malaysia, Sumatra, and Sri Lanka. In 1298, three years after his return, he was captured by the Genoese at the Battle of Curzola. While in a Genoa prison he met a Pisan scribe, Rusticello, to whom he dictated the popular *Description of the World* (now better known as *Il Milione*), an account of his 25 years in the Far East.

VENICE
how to organize your time

ITINERARIES

Distances in Venice are not great, but it still makes sense to see sights in self-contained clusters. Pay careful attention to opening times, especially those of churches (➤ 87). Should time run short, the sights marked with an asterisk could be skipped.

ITINERARY ONE	**SAN POLO**
Morning	Scuola Grande dei Carmini (➤ 26)
	Chiesa dei Carmini (➤ 26)
	San Sebastiano (➤ 25)
	San Nicolò dei Mendicoli * (➤ 53)
	San Pantalon (➤ 53)
	Santa Maria Gloriosa dei Frari (➤ 28)
Afternoon	Scuola Grande di San Rocco (➤ 27)
	San Polo (➤ 53)
	Campo San Polo (➤ 55)
	San Giacomo dell'Orio (➤ 52)
ITINERARY TWO	**SAN MARCO**
Morning	Ponte di Rialto and Rialto markets (➤ 81)
	Boat ride on Canal Grande to San Marco (➤ 24)
	Piazza San Marco (➤ 36)
	Campanile (➤ 38)
	Basilica di San Marco (➤ 39)
	Museo Civico Correr * (➤ 37)
Afternoon	Palazzo Ducale (➤ 40)
	San Zaccaria (➤ 45)
	San Giovanni in Bragora * (➤ 47)
	Boat (No. 82) to San Giorgio Maggiore (➤ 44)
	Boat (No. 82) from the Giudecca to Piazzale Roma
ITINERARY THREE	**CASTELLO**
Morning	Santa Maria Formosa (➤ 42)
	San Zaccaria (➤ 45)
	San Francesco della Vigna * (➤ 52)
	Scuola di San Giorgio degli Schiavoni (➤ 46)
	San Giovanni in Bragora * (➤ 47)

Afternoon	*Motoscafo* (No 52) from Tana to Murano (► 20)
	Return by boat to the Fondamente Nuove
	I Gesuiti * (► 52)
	Madonna dell'Orto (► 33)
	Santi Giovanni e Paolo (► 43)
	Santa Maria dei Miracoli (► 41)

ITINERARY FOUR — DORSODURO

Morning	Boat ride down the Canal Grande (► 24)
	Gallerie dell'Accademia (► 31)
	Santa Maria della Salute (► 34)

Afternoon	Collezione Peggy Guggenheim (► 32)
	Santo Stefano (► 30)
	Traghetto from San Samuele to Ca' Rezzonico
	Ca' Rezzonico * (► 29)
	Santa Maria Gloriosa dei Frari (► 28)

The Campanile and Palazzo Ducale

15

WALKS

The Rialto bridge

INFORMATION

FROM THE RIALTO TO PIAZZA SAN MARCO

Walk north from the Rialto bridge up Ruga degli Orefici. Turn left on Ruga Vecchia San Giovanni and follow it west to Campo San Polo. From the square's southwestern corner follow the alleys to Campo San Tomà. From here, head to Campo dei Frari and follow Calle Scaleter and Calle San Pantalon to Campo San Pantalon and Campo Santa Margherita. From the latter, either walk to Campo San Barnaba along Rio Terrà Canal, or loop west from Campo dei Carmini to take in San Sebastiano and perhaps San Nicolò dei Mendicoli. Return to Campo San Barnaba on Calle d'Avogaria and Calle Lunga San Barnaba, then follow Calle dei Casini and Calle della Toletta to the Accademia. Here you might divert south to the Zattere ai Gesuati and then east to Punta della Dogana, returning to the

Accademia via Santa Maria della Salute. Otherwise, cross the Ponte dell'Accademia to Campo Santo Stefano (Campo Francesco Morosini).

Walk east on Calle Spezier into Campo San Maurizio. Continue east to Campo San Moisè via Campo Santa Maria Zobenigo and Calle Larga (Viale) XXII Marzo. Beyond San Moisè, turn right down Calle Vallaresso and follow the waterfront east to Piazza San Marco.

Piazza San Marco

FROM PIAZZA SAN MARCO THROUGH THE CITY'S QUIETER NORTHERN DISTRICTS TO THE FERROVIA

Walk east from Piazza San Marco to Campo di San Zaccaria via either the Riva degli Schiavoni and Calle San Zaccaria, or Calle della Canonica and Campo SS Filippo e Giacomo. From the northwestern corner of Campo San Zaccaria, take Calle San Provolo north and then turn left on to Corte Rotta (this turns into Ruga Giuffa) to reach Campo Santa Maria Formosa. Take Calle Lunga Santa Maria Formosa off the eastern side of the square and follow it to Calle Ospedale and Salizzada SS Giovanni e Paolo. Turn left here to reach the church and Campo di SS Giovanni e Paolo. Proceed west on Calle Larga G Gallina to Campo Santa Maria Nova, detouring south briefly to see Santa Maria dei Miracoli.

Continue northwest through Campo San Canciano. Shortly before reaching Campo SS Apostoli, turn right on Calle Muazzo and Rio Terrà dei SS Apostoli toward Campo dei Gesuiti. Turn left to follow Fondamenta Zen west along the canal. Turn left at the end (Calle della Racchetta) and then take the third right (Sottopasseggio dei Preti).

Turn right on Fondamenta di San Felice and then left on to Fondamenta della Misericordia. At Calle Larga turn right to Campo dei Mori and Madonna dell'Orto. Return south to Fondamenta degli Ormesini and cross the Rio della Misericordia canal to reach Campo di Ghetto Nuovo, the heart of Venice's fascinating old Jewish ghetto. Explore the area and then head southwest to Fondamenta Pescaria. Cross the Canale di Cannaregio into Campo San Geremia and follow Rio Terrà di Lista di Spagna to the train station (Ferrovia).

THE SIGHTS

- Piazza San Marco (➤ 36)
- Palazzo Ducale (➤ 40)
- San Zaccaria (➤ 45)
- Santa Maria Formosa (➤ 42)
- Santi Giovanni e Paolo (➤ 43)
- Campo SS Giovanni e Paolo (➤ 54)
- Santa Maria dei Miracoli (➤ 41)
- I Gesuiti (➤ 52)
- Campo dei Mori (➤ 54)
- Madonna dell'Orto (➤ 33)

INFORMATION

Distance 2mi.
Time 2–4 hours
Start point Piazza San Marco
🚇 G12
🚤 San Marco 1, 3, 4, 82
End point Train station (Ferrovia)
🚇 D10
🚤 Ferrovia 1, 3, 4, 82
🕐 Opening hours vary considerably
🍴 Campo Santa Maria Formosa (➤ 55)

17

ROLLS

SAN MARCO

Recommending a particular evening stroll in Venice is not easy, for almost any combination of alleys and streets offers a magical and memorable experience. Water laps quietly in the canals, streets are mostly empty and deathly quiet (but perfectly safe), and every shadow hides a special secret. If you want some activity, however, and the promise of an aperitif at the end of your stroll, try walking from Piazza San Marco to Campo Santo Stefano (Campo Francesco Morosini). Exit the Piazza at the west end (or walk round by the water and the Giardinetti Reali) and follow Calle Larga (Viale) XXII Marzo and Calle delle Ostreghe to Campo Santa Maria Zobenigo. Then walk through Campo San Maurizio into Campo Santo Stefano (Campo Francesco Morosini), where you can either take time out at Paolin (► 75) or walk to the Ponte dell'Accademia for views of the Grand Canal and the Salute.

SAN POLO

Start at the Ponte di Rialto by admiring the streetlife of the Rialto: day-trippers returning home, people crowding into waterside restaurants, and the constant coming and going of gondolas. Then walk west along the Fondamenta del Vin and turn right through Campo San Silvestro to Campo Sant'Aponal. From here, turn left along Calle di Mezzo to Campo San Polo, one of Venice's largest squares, where the chances are there will be people doing much the same as you are (several bars here have outside tables so that their patrons can watch the world go by). Next, take Salizzada San Polo and follow the streets west to Campo San Tomà. Turn north toward the Frari and then west toward San Pantalon. From here, walk over the bridge into Campo Santa Margherita, another lively square with several pleasant bars and cafés (► 54–55).

INFORMATION

San Marco
Distance 0.3mi.
Time 10–15 minutes
Start point Riva degli Schiavoni or Piazza San Marco
➕ G/H12
🚤 San Marco or San Zaccaria 1, 3, 4, 52, 82
End point Campo Santo Stefano (Campo Francesco Morosini) or Ponte dell'Accademia
➕ F12/E13
🚤 Accademia 1, 3, 4, 82

San Polo
Distance 0.8mi.
Time 20–25 minutes
Start point Ponte di Rialto
➕ G11
🚤 Rialto 1, 3, 82
End point Campo Santa Margherita
➕ D12
🚤 Ca' Rezzonico 1

Santa Maria della Salute at sunset

ORGANIZED SIGHTSEEING

AMERICAN EXPRESS TOURS

Although several firms offer organized sightseeing tours, the best-known trips are arranged by American Express, whose office lies close to Piazza San Marco (✚ G12 ✉ Salizzada San Moisè, San Marco 1471 ☎ 520 0844). Currently the company offers two basic city tours daily, one in the morning and the other in the afternoon. The tours last two hours and cost around L35,000 each, with a reduction if you book for both. Trips start from outside the American Express office, though you should call ahead to confirm current prices and timings.

The morning tour is known as the "Jewels of the Venetian Republic Tour" and visits, among other sights, the Basilica di San Marco, the Campanile, and the Palazzo Ducale. The second tour visits several palaces and churches, including the Frari, and ends at the Rialto bridge after a gondola ride to the Ca' d'Oro. American Express also offers an evening tour, the "Evening Serenade" (twice nightly), which involves a ride in a gondola with musicians and singers, and departs from Piazza Santa Maria del Giglio. It also runs, along with several other companies, much more expensive trips to the mainland towns of Padua and Asolo, as well as boat and coach trips to see the Palladian villas dotted along the Brenta Canal. These should be booked a day in advance.

Another tour heads out to the Venetian lagoon and islands, a three-hour trip with two departures daily (morning and afternoon) which takes in Murano, Torcello, and Burano. Tours depart from the Riva degli Schiavoni. On the whole it is best to avoid some of the other commercialized tours, especially to Murano, as overdue emphasis is often placed on visiting glass factories with a view to selling you their products. You might consider Cooperativa San Marco tours, which can be booked through travel agents or direct from the booth on the dockside by the Giardinetti Reali.

Guides

Venice has numerous multilingual guides who can be hired by the half-day, full day or week, as well as gondoliers and drivers for hire. American Express (see main text) organizes both guides and gondoliers, or you can choose one yourself by contacting the Guides' Association (✚ G11 ✉ Calle Sant'Antonio 5448a, Castello ☎ 523 9902). The main tourist office in the Palazzetto Selva (➤ 87) also has details of guides, as well as information on organized tours. Bookings for trips usually have to be made directly or through travel agents, of which there are many dotted around the city.

Bound for one of the islands of the lagoon

EXCURSIONS

Murano glass

INFORMATION

Murano

➕ H–N/4–7

✉ Museo Vetrario: Palazzo
   Giustinian, Fondamenta
   Giustinian. SS Maria e
   Donato: Fondamenta
   Giustinian

☎ Museo Vetrario: 739 586.
   SS Maria e Donato: 739 056

🕐 Museo Vetrario: Thu–Tue
   10–5. SS Maria e Donato:
   daily 8–12, 4–6:30

🚤 52 (frequent) or 12 (every
   60–90 minutes) from
   Fondamente Nuove

♿ Museo Vetrario: moderate.
   SS Maria e Donato: free

❓ Murano lies 1km north of
   Venice; the boat trip takes
   seven minutes. Disembark
   from the No. 52 at Colonna for
   the Fondamenta dei Vetrai and
   San Pietro Martire

Burano

➕ H–N/1–2

✉ Scuola dei Merletti: Piazza
   Baldassare Galuppi

☎ Scuola dei Merletti: 730 034

🕐 Scuola dei Merletti Tue–Sat
   9–6, Sun 10–4

🚤 12 from the Fondamente
   Nuove (every 60–90 minutes)

♿ Scuola dei Merletti: moderate

❓ Burano lies about 4.5mi.
   north-east of Venice; the boat
   ride takes 40–50 minutes

MURANO

Murano is known primarily for its glass, since Venice moved its glass furnaces to the island in 1291 as a precaution against fire. Though not as pretty as the lagoon's other major islands (see below for Burano and Torcello), it has three major sights over and above its ubiquitous glass workshops and showrooms (most of the latter are on the island's main street, Fondamenta dei Vetrai). The first is the church of San Pietro Martire, noted for the superb wooden carvings (1652–1656) in its sacristy and Giovanni Bellini's glorious altarpiece (second altar on the right) of the *Madonna and Child with Doge Barbarigo and Sts. Mark and Augustine* (1488). Also well worth seeing is the Museo Vetrario, Italy's only glass museum, with displays dating from Roman times to the present day. Just beyond lies the church of SS Maria e Donato, its exterior distinguished by a striking arched and colonnaded apse. Inside, the 12th-century apse mosaic of the Madonna is outstanding, as are the swirling colored patterns of the lovely mosaic floor (1141).

BURANO

If Murano is known for its glass, Burano is equally lauded for its lace. Breathtakingly intricate examples of traditional lace can be seen in the Scuola dei Merletti, which also allows you to watch local women working according to the old methods. Unlike Murano, Burano is attractive to visit for its own sake. The island's fame in part rests on its many brightly colored houses, whose wonderful primary colors make its streets and canals as picturesque as any in Venice itself.

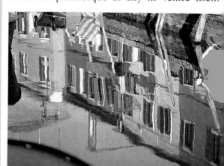

Fishing boats are still moored at the island's fringes, while nets are laid out on the sidewalks to dry, features which—despite the faint air of commercialism and the many visitors—still lend the island the feel of a genuine fishing community. At little less than half a mile across, the island is also easy to explore, and as a day trip it makes the perfect accompaniment to Torcello, which lies just five minutes away by boat (see below).

Torcello

TORCELLO

Torcello is one of the most magical places in Venice. Although now an all but deserted island, it was probably the city's birthplace and the first area of the lagoon settled in the 5th century. Malaria and the silting up of its canals snuffed out its prosperity in the 12th century, double blows from which it never recovered. Today, the island is home to little more than a single hamlet and a beautiful patchwork of green fields and tree-shaded canals. Dominating its huddle of houses is the cathedral of Santa Maria Assunta, Venice's oldest building (founded 639). The cathedral is one of Venice's loveliest sights and is the finest Veneto-Byzantine church in Italy. The simple interior is filled with outstanding works of art, chief of which are the 12th-century apse mosaic of the Madonna (the 11th-century frieze below shows the Apostles) and the graphic 12th-century mosaic of the *Last Judgment* on the rear wall. Almost equally remarkable are the 7th-century high altar, the 11th-century mosaics to its right, and the beautiful rood screen and choir, the former supporting a painted balcony of the *Virgin and Apostles*. Also worth seeing close by are the Byzantine church of Santa Fosca—beautiful if rather over-restored—and the small Museo dell'Estuario, a museum whose exhibits are devoted to the area's long history.

INFORMATION

Torcello

➕ Off map

☎ Santa Maria Assunta and Santa Fosca: 730 084. Museo dell'Estuario: 730 761

🕐 Santa Maria Assunta and Santa Fosca: daily 10–12:30, 2–5. Museo dell'Estuario: Tue–Sun 10:30–12:30, 2–5

🚤 12 from the Fondamente Nuove (every 60–90 minutes)

🎫 Santa Maria Assunta: inexpensive. Santa Fosca: free. Museo dell'Estuario: inexpensive

❓ Torcello lies 5mi. northeast of Venice; the boat ride takes 45 minutes. Catch the first boat of the day to avoid the crowds

Practicalities

The *Biglietto Isole*, a single one-way ticket, enables you to visit Murano, Burano, and Torcello with stopovers *en route*, though a less expensive additional ticket is required for the return to Venice from either Burano or Torcello. Boats usually stop at Burano first, except early in the morning and during weekends in the high season, when they dock at Torcello. If returning to Venice from Torcello, check that the boat is returning directly to the city rather than taking a longer route home via Treponti, Punta Sabbioni, and the Lido. Burano has several good restaurants and many bars and cafés, while Torcello has one expensive restaurant, a middling trattoria, and two small bars (➤ 68–76), but there are plenty of picnic spots.

WHAT'S ON

FEBRUARY	*Carnevale* (*Carnival*): pageants, masks, and costumes (ten days leading up to Shrove Tuesday).
MARCH	*Su e zo per i ponti*: a long street race for serious and fun runners alike in which competitors run "up and down the bridges" of Venice (second Sunday of the month).
APRIL	*Festa di San Marco*: the feast day of Venice's patron saint is marked by a gondola race from Sant'Elena to the Punta della Dogana. Men traditionally give women a red rose.
MAY	*La Sensa*: Venice's mayor reenacts the Marriage to the Sea, in which the doge would cast a ring into the sea to symbolize the "wedding" of the city to the sea (Sunday after Ascension Day).
	Vogalonga: literally the "long row," a 20 mile race from Piazza San Marco to Burano and back; many hundreds of different boats take part (Sunday following La Sensa).
JUNE	*Biennale*: Venice's international art exhibition takes place every odd-numbered year (June–September).
JULY	*Festa del Redentore*: pontoons are laid across the Giudecca canal to the Redentore to celebrate Venice's deliverance from the plague of 1576. People picnic in boats and there is a fireworks display (third Sunday of the month).
SEPTEMBER	*Venice Film Festival*: international festival held on the Lido (early September).
	Regata Storica: historical costume pageant and procession of boats on the Canal Grande, followed by a race between gondoliers and other oarsmen (first Sunday of the month).
NOVEMBER	*Festa della Salute*: a pontoon is built across the Canal Grande to the Salute to celebrate the passing of a plague in 1630 (November 21).

VENICE's
top 25 sights

The sights are shown on the maps on the inside front cover and inside back cover, and are numbered **1–25** from west to east across the city.

1

CANAL GRANDE

INFORMATION

- C–G/10–13
- 1, 82 (year round); 3, 4 (summer only)
- Good
- Moderate
- Scuola Grande di San Rocco (➤ 27), Santa Maria Gloriosa dei Frari (➤ 28), Ca' Rezzonico (➤ 29), Gallerie dell'Accademia (➤ 31), Ca d'Oro (➤ 35), Piazza San Marco (➤ 36)
- Vaporetto 1 halts at every stop; 82 stops at Piazzale Roma, Ferrovia, San Marcuola, the Rialto, San Tomà, San Samuele, and the Accademia; 3 stops at the Rialto, San Samuele, and Accademia; and 4 stops at the Accademia and San Samuele

Regata Storica

"*There's no better introduction to the magic of Venice than a boat trip down the Grand Canal, an endlessly unfolding pageant that offers superb views of the city's finest palaces and a fascinating insight into Venetian daily life.***"**

Bustle The Grand Canal is the world's most beautiful street. Snaking 2.5 miles through the heart of Venice, it divides the city: three of the city's six districts, or *sestieri*, lie to one side and three to the other. At most hours of the day and night it is alive with boats and bustle of all description, providing an almost hypnotic spectacle when admired from one of its three bridges (the Scalzi, Rialto, and Accademia) or from the heavily laden *vaporetti* that ply up and down its length. In addition to the life of the canal is the attraction of the palaces that line its banks, a 500-year-old digest of the city's most appealing architecture.

Boats A trip along the canal is a pleasure in itself, and one that you can never tire of. The best thing to do is to board either *vaporetto* No. 1 or No. 82 at Piazzale Roma or the Ferrovia (train station), making sure the boat is heading in the right direction. Try to secure one of the handful of outside seats at the front or rear of the boat (Venetians prefer to stand in the middle). The Rialto and Accademia bridges make convenient breaks in the ride, but for your first trip it is worth staying aboard all the way to San Marco (and perhaps doing the return trip to take in the palaces on the opposite bank). It is also well worth making the trip at night, when the experience, if anything, is even more magical.

SAN SEBASTIANO

❝*While paintings by some of Venice's artists—notably Titian and Tintoretto—are often showcased in grandiose settings, the city's finest collection of works by Veronese is gathered in the humble little church of San Sebastiano.*❞

Veronese Born in Verona, Veronese (1528–1588) moved to Venice while he was in his twenties, settling close to San Sebastiano, which soon became his parish church. In 1555 he was commissioned to decorate the church's sacristy, where he left paintings of the *Evangelists* and the *Coronation of the Virgin*. Impressed by his work, the church authorities gave him free rein to decorate the church's ceiling, and he produced a sumptuous collection of paintings, gilt, and elaborate stucco (much of the decoration was carried out by Veronese's brother, Benedetto). The three main panels depict episodes from the Old Testament story of Esther, chosen for its symbolic parallels with the stories of Eve and the Virgin Mary.

Monopoly The hand of Veronese can also be seen in the choir, where he painted the high altarpiece —the *Madonna and Child with Sts. Sebastian, Peter, Francis, and Catherine* (1570)—and the two vast paintings on the left and right walls. The latter portray *Sts. Mark and Marcellinus Led to Martyrdom and Comforted by St. Sebastian* and *The Second Martyrdom of St. Sebastian* (Sebastian survived his first assault by arrows and was martyred by being pummeled to death). Veronese also painted *The Trial and Martyrdom of St. Sebastian* in the nuns' choir, an unusual gallery above the church's west end. He even designed the organ and painted its door panels, his decorative monopoly of San Sebastiano making it only fitting that he was buried here: his tomb, and that of his brother, lie in front of the chapel to the left of the choir.

HIGHLIGHTS

- Sacristy
- Ceiling
- Nuns' choir
- Choir
- Organ
- *St. Nicholas* (1563), Titian (first chapel on right)
- *Madonna and Child* (16th century), Tommaso Lombardo (second chapel on right)
- *Tomb of Archbishop Podocattaro of Cyprus* (d. 1555), Sansovino (fourth chapel on right)

INFORMATION

- ✚ C13
- ✉ Campo San Sebastiano
- ☎ 282 487
- 🕐 Daily 10–2, 4–6
- 🍴 Campo Santa Margherita and Campo San Barnaba
- 🚏 San Basilio 82
- ♿ Good
- 🎫 Free
- ↔ Scuola Grande dei Carmini (➤ 26), Scuola Grande di San Rocco (➤ 27), Santa Maria Gloriosa dei Frari (➤ 28), Ca' Rezzonico (➤ 29), Gallerie dell'Accademia (➤ 31)
- ❓ Restoration work or staff shortages may alter opening times

3

SCUOLA GRANDE DEI CARMINI

"Giovanni Battista Tiepolo's paintings are not to all tastes, but those in the intimate little Scuola Grande dei Carmini —all pastel shades and fleshy figures—are a pleasant change from the more obvious drama of Titian or Tintoretto."

Carmelites The Carmelite Order's Venetian chapter was originally installed in Santa Maria del Carmelo (or Carmini), the Carmelite church just to the left of the *scuola* (see below). In 1667 the order commissioned Baldassare Longhena, one of the era's leading architects, to design a new home in the present building (Longhena also designed Santa Maria della Salute and a number of palaces on the Grand Canal). The façade, though hampered by its cramped site, is known for its rigorous symmetry and many masks and projections, all favored by architects of the period.

Paintings The highlights are Giovanni Battista Tiepolo's nine ceiling paintings (1739–1744) in the Salone, a large room on the second floor reached via an extravagantly stuccoed staircase. The paintings' central panel depicts the vision of St. Simon Stock (elected the Carmelites' prior-general in 1247), in which the Virgin appears to the saint with a "scapular." This garment of two linked pieces of cloth became central to Carmelite belief as wearers were promised relief from the pains of purgatory on the "first Sunday after death." Two adjacent rooms, the Albergo and Archivio, feature heavy wooden ceilings and several paintings, the best of which is Piazzetta's *Judith and Holofernes* (1743). Be sure to visit the Chiesa dei Carmini to see Lorenzo Lotto's *St. Nicholas of Bari* (1529), located by the side door (second chapel), and Cima da Conegliano's fine *Nativity* (1509) above the second altar on the opposite (south) wall.

SCUOLA GRANDE DI SAN ROCCO

"In a city of superlative and often striking works of art, none made such a marked and powerful first impression than the colossal cycle of 54 paintings by Tintoretto that line the walls of the Scuola Grande di San Rocco."

Scuola This *scuola*, formerly a charitable institution for the sick, was founded in 1478 in honor of St. Roch, a saint whose efficacy against disease made him popular in pestilence-ridden Venice. In 1564, having become one of the city's wealthiest fraternities, the *scuola* instigated a competition to decorate the walls of its meeting place. It was won by Tintoretto, who then spent some 23 years creating one of Europe's greatest painting cycles.

Albergo To see Tintoretto's 54 paintings in the order they were painted, ignore the canvases on the ground floor and in the main hall (Sala Grande) up the stairs. Instead, go to the Sala dell'Albergo (off the main hall), dominated by a huge *Crucifixion* (1565), often described as one of Italy's greatest paintings. The room's central ceiling panel is *St. Roch in Glory*, the painting that won Tintoretto his commission.

In the main hall are ceiling paintings (1575–1581) describing episodes from the Old Testament, all carefully chosen to draw parallels with the *scuola*'s charitable or curative aims. The ten wall paintings show scenes from the New Testament. Note the superb 17th-century wooden carvings around the walls, by the little-known sculptor Francesco Pianta. Of the eight paintings downstairs, the artist's last in the *scuola* (1583–1588), the best are the idiosyncratic *Annunciation* and *The Flight into Egypt*.

HIGHLIGHTS

- Crucifixion
- Moses Strikes Water from the Rock
- The Fall of Manna
- The Temptation of Christ
- The Adoration of the Shepherds
- Wooden sculptures
- The Flight into Egypt
- Annunciation

Tintoretto's Crucifixion

INFORMATION

- E11
- Campo San Rocco
- 523 4864
- Daily. Apr–Oct: 9–5:30. Nov–Mar: Mon–Fri 10–1; Sat–Sun 10–4
- Campo dei Frari
- San Tomà 1, 82
- Poor
- Moderate
- San Sebastiano (➤ 25), Scuola Grande dei Carmini (➤ 26), Santa Maria Gloriosa dei Frari (➤ 28), Accademia (➤ 31)
- A free leaflet to the *scuola*'s paintings is usually available with your ticket.

27

5

SANTA MARIA GLORIOSA DEI FRARI

HIGHLIGHTS

- *Madonna and Child*, Giovanni Bellini
- *Assumption*, Titian
- *Madonna di Ca' Pesaro*, Titian
- *Madonna and Child* (1339), Paolo Veneziano (sacristy)
- *St. John the Baptist*, Donatello
- *Mausoleo Tiziano* (Tomb of Titian)
- *Monumento a Iacopo Marcello* (d. 1484)
- Wooden choir (124 stalls)
- *Monumento al Doge Giovanni Pesaro* (d. 1659)
- *Monumento al Canova*

INFORMATION

- ✚ E11
- ✉ Campo dei Frari
- ☎ 522 2637
- 🕐 Mon–Sat 9:30–12, 2:30–6; Sun 3–6
- 🍴 Campo dei Frari
- 🚤 San Tomà 1, 82
- ♿ Good: one or two steps
- 🎫 Inexpensive; free on Sun
- ↔ San Sebastiano (► 25), Scuola Grande dei Carmini (► 26), Scuola Grande di San Rocco (► 27), Ca' Rezzonico (► 29), Gallerie dell'Accademia (► 31)

"*If you were allowed to walk away with just one work of art from Venice it could well be Giovanni Bellini's sublime altarpiece in Santa Maria Gloriosa dei Frari— although two other paintings in this magnificent Gothic church are contenders.***"**

Church The "Frari" narrowly outranks SS Giovanni e Paolo as Venice's largest and most important church. Founded around 1250, it became the mother church of the city's Franciscans, after whom it is named—*frari* is a Venetian corruption of *frati*, meaning "friars."

Tombs Many of the city's great and good are buried in the church, among them the painter Titian (d. 1576), whose 19th-century tomb occupies the second altar on the right (south) wall. Opposite, on the left wall, stands the *Monumento al Canova* (1827), an unmistakable marble pyramid that contains the sculptor's heart. To its right lies the wonderfully gaudy tomb of Doge Giovanni Pesaro (d. 1659). The composer Claudio Monteverdi (d. 1643) is buried in the third chapel to the left of the high altar.

Art The Frari's most striking painting is Titian's *Assumption* (1516–1518), its position above the high altar designed to attract your attention from most of the church. The same painter's influential *Madonna di Ca' Pesaro* (1526), on the last altar of the left aisle, is almost equally captivating. The church's most beautiful work of art, however, is Giovanni Bellini's sublime triptych of the *Madonna and Child between Sts. Nicholas, Peter, Mark, and Benedict* (1488), located in the sacristy off the right transept. In the first chapel on the right of the high altar is Donatello's statue of *St. John the Baptist* (1438), the only work in Venice by the famous Florentine sculptor.

CA' REZZONICO

"Gazing at the Grand Canal's palaces from a boat you can't help but wish you could see inside some of them, which is the attraction of Ca' Rezzonico, a museum that re-creates a Venetian palace as it might have appeared in the 18th century."

Palace The Ca' Rezzonico was begun in 1667 by Baldassare Longhena, one of the leading architects of his day, but remained half-finished following the ruin of its owner, Filippo Bon. In 1751 the shell was bought by the Rezzonico family, a *nouveau riche* clan, and then passed through several hands (including the son of poet Robert Browning) before opening as a museum in 1936. It begins in fine style with a sumptuous ballroom decorated with *trompe-l'œil* and enormous chandeliers. Highlights of subsequent rooms include ceiling frescoes by G.B. Tiepolo, some fine lacquerwork, Flemish tapestries, and pastel portraits by Rosalba Carriera.

Paintings Much of the palace's third floor is devoted to a picture gallery, whose highlight is a pair of paintings by Canaletto, two of only a handful that remain on public display in Venice. Also of interest are Francesco Guardi's views of the city's convents and gambling rooms, together with 34 amateurish but fascinating portraits of Venetian life by Pietro Longhi, among them his well-known *Rhinoceros*, painted during the animal's stay in Venice in 1779. Rooms off to the right include a splendid bedchamber, complete with 18th-century closet and sponge bag. The final rooms contain the museum's pictorial high point, a series of satirical frescoes (1793–1797) by G.D. Tiepolo. The fourth floor offers puppets, a reconstructed 18th-century pharmacy and fine views.

HIGHLIGHTS

- Ballroom
- GB Tiepolo ceiling frescoes
- Carriera portraits
- Lacquerwork
- Gondola cabin, or *felze* (ground floor)
- Canaletto paintings
- Francesco Guardi paintings
- Pietro Longhi paintings
- Bedchamber
- GD Tiepolo satirical frescoes

INFORMATION

- ✚ E12
- ✉ Fondamenta Rezzonico
- ☎ 241 0100
- 🕐 Apr–Sep: Sat–Thu 9–5. Oct–Mar: Sat–Thu 10–4
- 🚌 Campo San Barnaba
- ⛴ Ca' Rezzonico 1
- Poor: steps to upper floors
- Expensive
- San Sebastiano (➤ 25), Scuola Grande dei Carmini (➤ 26), Scuola Grande di San Rocco (➤ 27), Santa Maria Gloriosa dei Frari (➤ 28), Gallerie dell'Accademia (➤ 31), Collezione Peggy Guggenheim (➤ 32)

A gondola cabin, or felze

SANTO STEFANO

The leaning bell tower of Santo Stefano

❝ *Savor the sensation of walking from the heat and bustle of a city into a building which induces immediate calm, an effect that is soon gained by the soothing Gothic interior of Santo Stefano, one of Venice's loveliest churches.* ❞

Santo Stefano sits on the edge of Campo Santo Stefano (also known as Campo Francesco Morosini), one of Venice's most charming squares; the nearby Paolin is an ideal place to sit with a drink or ice cream (➤ 75). The church has not always been so peaceful, having been reconsecrated six times to wash away the stain of blood spilled by murders within its walls. Today, its interior is overarched by an exquisite "ship's keel" ceiling and framed by tie beams and pillars of Greek and red Veronese marble.

Tombs At the center of the nave lies Doge Francesco Morosini (d. 1612, and buried under Venice's largest tomb slab), famous for recapturing the Peloponnese and blowing up the Parthenon with a single shot. Other tombs command attention, notably Pietro Lombardo's *Monument to Giacomo Surian* (d. 1493) on the wall to the right of the main door, but the church's chief artistic interest lies in the gloomy sacristy at the end of the right nave. The altar wall features two narrow-framed *Saints* by Bartolomeo Vivarini, as well as a recessed 13th-century Byzantine icon. On the walls to either side are four paintings by Tintoretto and four portraits of Augustinian cardinals (Santo Stefano is an Augustinian church).

GALLERIE DELL'ACCADEMIA

"*An art gallery is almost superfluous in a city where art awaits you at every turn, but no trip to Venice would be complete without a trip to the Accademia, home to the world's greatest collection of Venetian paintings.***"**

History The Accademia began life as Venice's art school in 1750, moving to its present site in 1807, when it garnered much of its permanent collection from churches and religious houses suppressed by Napoleonic decree. Its paintings, arranged chronologically, spread across 24 rooms.

Paintings Some of the gallery's best-known paintings are found in the first five rooms, Room 1 opening with Byzantine works, a style that influenced the city's earliest painters. Rooms 2–5 contain canvases by Carpaccio, Mantegna, Bellini, and others, reflecting Venice's Renaissance heyday, as well as the Accademia's most famous painting, Giorgione's mysterious *Tempest*. Rooms 10 and 11 feature High Renaissance masterpieces, such as Veronese's luxuriant *Supper in the House of Levi* and Tintoretto's iconoclastic *Miracle of the Slave* and *The Translation of the Body of St. Mark*.

Cycles Leave plenty of time for the Accademia's highlights, two *storie* or fresco cycles (rooms 20 and 21). The first, "The Miracles of the True Cross" (1494–1510), was painted by a variety of artists for the Scuola di San Giovanni Evangelista. Each describes a miracle worked by a relic of the "True Cross" owned by the *scuola*, though often the miracle itself takes second place to the fascinating anecdotal detail. The same is true for the second cycle, painted by Carpaccio for the Scuola di Sant'Orsola, with episodes from the "Life of St. Ursula."

HIGHLIGHTS

- *Coronation of the Virgin* (c. 1345), Paolo Veneziano (Room 1)
- *Presentation of Jesus in the Temple*, Carpaccio (Room 2)
- *Madonna and Saints* (c. 1485), Giovanni Bellini (Room 2)
- *Tempest* (c. 1500), Giorgione (Room 5)
- *Supper in the House of Levi* (1573), Veronese (Room 10)
- *The Translation of the Body of St. Mark* (c. 1560), Tintoretto (Room 10)
- *Pietà* (c. 1576), Titian (Room 10)
- Pietro Longhi paintings (Room 17)
- "The Miracles of the True Cross" (Room 20)
- "Life of St. Ursula" (c. 1490– 1496), Carpaccio (Room 21)

INFORMATION

- ✚ E13
- ✉ Campo della Carità
- ☎ 522 2247
- 🕐 Mon–Sat 9–7, Sun 9–2
- 🚏 Campo Santo Stefano (Campo Francesco Morosini)
- 🚤 Accademia 1, 3, 4, 82
- ♿ Poor: some steps
- 💲 Very expensive
- ↔ Santo Stefano (➤ 30), Collezione Peggy Guggenheim (➤ 32), Santa Maria della Salute (➤ 34)
- ❓ Arrive early to avoid lines, especially on Sun

9

COLLEZIONE PEGGY GUGGENHEIM

HIGHLIGHTS

- Garden
- The New Wing
- Henry Moore sculptures
- *Bird in Space*, Constantin Brancusi
- *Red Tower*, De Chirico
- *Robing of the Bride*, Max Ernst
- Silver bedhead, Alexander Calder
- Jackson Pollock paintings
- *The Poet*, Pablo Picasso
- *Angel of the Citadel*, Marino Marini

INFORMATION

- F13
- Palazzo Venier dei Leoni, Calle San Cristoforo
- 520 6288
- Easter–Oct: Wed–Mon 11–6, Sat 6–9
- Salute 1
- Good
- Expensive
- Ca' Rezzonico (➤ 29), Santo Stefano (➤ 30), Gallerie dell'Accademia (➤ 31), Santa Maria della Salute (➤ 34)

66 *It's rather apt that the Accademia and Guggenheim, Venice's two most visited galleries, are so close together, juxtaposing two matchless collections of paintings and sculptures—one traditional, one modern.* **99**

Palace The Guggenheim's small but polished collection was accumulated by Peggy Guggenheim (1898–1979), daughter of an American copper magnate, and installed by her in the 18th-century Palazzo Venier dei Leoni. The collection's appeal owes much to its immaculate presentation as well as to the beauty of its setting, many of the sculptures being arranged in a lovely garden. This has works by Henry Moore, Paolozzi, Giacometti, and others, and houses the New Wing and appealing "Museum Store."

Gallery Guggenheim's taste and money allowed her to select high-quality works from virtually every modern-art movement of the 20th century. At the same time she had a penchant for the surreal and avant-garde, having enjoyed a brief relationship with the Surrealist painter Max Ernst. The collection features Cubist works by Picasso and Braque, and the Surrealism of Dali, Magritte, and Mirò. American modernists include Jackson Pollock, de Kooning, and Rothko, while the English are represented by Francis Bacon. There are also sculptures by Calder and Brancusi, as well as works by Italians, notably the Futurists Balla and Boccioni. The most memorable work, however, is Marino Marini's provocative *Angel of the Citadel*, on the terrace overlooking the Grand Canal.

Angel of the Citadel

10

MADONNA DELL'ORTO

"*Madonna dell'Orto ranks high among Venetian churches, its lovely setting (well off the tourist trail) and graceful red-brick façade complemented by an airy interior that is filled with appealing works of art.*"

Exterior The first church on the present site was founded in 1350 and dedicated to St. Christopher, a statue of whom still dominates the lovely brick and marble façade. The sculpture was commissioned by the Merchants' Guild, whose altar to the saint (their patron) lay within the church. The building was rededicated to the Virgin in 1377, an act that was inspired by a miracle-working statue of the Madonna found in a nearby vegetable garden (*orto*). The elegant doorway, by Bartolomeo Bon, is a Renaissance-tinged work that departs from the façade's predominantly Gothic inspiration. Note the onion dome of the campanile, clear witness to the Byzantine influence on Venetian architecture.

Interior The artistic highlights begin above the first altar on the right, which features Cima da Conegliano's *St. John the Baptist* (1493). At the end of the right nave, above the door, stands Tintoretto's dramatic *Presentation of the Virgin* (1551). In the chapel to the right of the choir lies Tintoretto's tomb, together with those of his children, Domenico and Marietta, both painters themselves (Madonna dell'Orto was the family's parish church). A wall separates the artist from two of his finest paintings, the choir's grand *Last Judgment* and *The Making of the Golden Calf*. Of the three paintings in the apse to the rear, those on the right and left—the *Beheading of St. Paul* and *St. Peter's Vision of the Cross*—are by Tintoretto; the central *Annunciation* is by Palma il Giovane. Four of the five *Virtues* above are also by Tintoretto.

HIGHLIGHTS

- Façade
- Doorway
- *St. Christopher*, Nicolò di Giovanni
- Campanile
- *St. John the Baptist*, Cima da Conegliano
- *Presentation of the Virgin*, Tintoretto
- *The Making of the Golden Calf*, Tintoretto
- *Last Judgment*, Tintoretto
- *St. Agnes Raising Licinius*, Tintoretto (Cappella Contarini)

INFORMATION

- F8/9
- Campo Madonna dell'Orto
- 719 933
- Daily. Summer: 9:30–12, 4–6. Winter: 9:30–12, 3:30–5:30
- Madonna dell'Orto 52
- Good
- Free
- Ca' d'Oro (► 35), Campo dei Mori (► 54)

Red-brick façade of the Madonna dell'Orto

33

11

SANTA MARIA DELLA SALUTE

HIGHLIGHTS

- Exterior
- Marble floor
- *Descent of the Holy Spirit*, Titian
- *The Virgin Casting out the Plague*, Juste le Court
- *Feast at Cana* (1561), Tintoretto (sacristy)
- *Cain and Abel* (1542–1544), Titian (sacristy)
- *David and Goliath* (1542–1544), Titian (sacristy)
- *Sacrifice of Abraham* (1542–1544), Titian (sacristy)
- *St. Mark Enthroned between Sts. Cosmas, Damian, Roch, and Sebastian* (1510), Titian (sacristy)
- *Madonna*, Palma il Vecchio

INFORMATION

- F13
- Campo della Salute
- 522 5558
- Daily 9–12, 3–5
- Salute 1
- Poor: several steps
- Church: free. Sacristy: inexpensive
- Ca' Rezzonico (➤ 29), Santo Stefano (➤ 30), Gallerie dell'Accademia (➤ 31), Collezione Peggy Guggenheim (➤ 32)

The Salute's interior

"*In a city where almost every street and canal offers a memorable vista, the church of Santa Maria della Salute, proudly situated at the entrance to the Grand Canal, forms part of the panorama most people readily associate with Venice.***"**

Plague In 1630 Venice found itself ravaged by a plague so severe that the Senate promised to build a church in honor of the Virgin if she could save the city. Within weeks the pestilence had abated, and on April 1 the following year the first stone of the Salute, which means both "health" and "salvation," was laid. Its architect, chosen after a competition, was Baldassare Longhena, responsible for a host of outstanding Venetian buildings. His design proved to be a baroque model for years to come, combining the Palladian influence of his master, Scamozzi (Palladio's closest follower), with a range of personal innovations.

Interior The Salute's main impact is as a distant prospect, its dazzling exterior detail and great dome (modelled on that of St. Peter's in Rome) forming irreplaceable elements of the Venetian skyline. The church's interior is more restrained, and its fine marble floor is the first thing that catches your eye. Moving left from the side entrance, the third of the three altars boasts an early painting by Titian, the *Descent of the Holy Spirit* (1550). The high altar supports *The Virgin Casting out the Plague* (1670), a magnificent sculpture designed by Longhena and carved by Juste le Court. The supplicant figure on the left represents Venice, while the elderly harridan moving off to the right symbolizes the plague. It is well worth paying to see the sacristy, which contains paintings by Titian and Tintoretto.

CA' D'ORO

❝ *The smaller and less famous galleries of a city are often more rewarding than some of the bigger attractions. The Ca' d'Oro is no exception: its collection of paintings, sculptures, and* objets d'art *is one of the most absorbing in Venice.*❞

Palace The Ca' d'Oro, or "House of Gold," takes its name from the gilding that once covered its façade, a decorative veneer now worn away by wind and rain. The façade remains one of the most accomplished pieces of Venetian-Byzantine architecture in the city.

The same, sadly, cannot be said of the interior, which has been ravaged by a succession of hapless owners. The palace passed to the state in 1916.

Gallery The gallery divides into two floors, each of these arranged around a central *portego* (see panel ➤ 57). On the second floor a captivating polyptych of the *Crucifixion* by Antonio Vivarini greets you, along with sculptural fragments belonging to the *Massacre of the Innocents* (14th century). Moving right you come to the gallery's pictorial masterpiece, Mantegna's somber *St. Sebastian* (1506). To its left, in the *portego*, is a pair of busts by Tullio Lombardo (15th century), followed by six bronze reliefs by Andrea Briscio (1470–1532). Rooms off the *portego* contain medallions, a *Madonna* by Giovanni Bellini, and Florentine and Sienese paintings. Upstairs are tapestries, paintings by Titian, Van Dyck, and Tintoretto, and damaged frescoes by Pordenone, Titian, and Giorgione.

HIGHLIGHTS

- Grand Canal façade
- *Massacre of the Innocents*, artist unknown
- *Crucifixion*, Antonio Vivarini
- Three-dimensional *paliotto* with *Scenes from the Life of St. Catherine* (16th century), artist unknown
- *St. Sebastian*, Andrea Mantegna
- *Man and Woman*, busts by Tullio Lombardo
- *The Story of the True Cross*, bronze reliefs by Andrea Briscio
- *Madonna of the Beautiful Eyes*, Giovanni Bellini
- *Flagellation*, Luca Signorelli
- *Scenes from the Life of Lucrezia*, Biagio d'Antonio

The Ca' d'Oro's ornate façade

INFORMATION

35

13

PIAZZA SAN MARCO

INFORMATION

- G12
- Museo Archeologico: 522 5978. Libreria Sansoviniana: 520 8788
- Museo Archeologico: daily 9–2. Libreria Sansoviniana: by appointment only Mon–Sat 9–1; contact the Bibliotecca Marciana next door at No 7
- Florian (➤ 74) and Quadri (➤ 75)
- San Marco or San Zaccaria 1, 52, 82
- Good
- Museo Archeologico: moderate
- Museo Civico Correr (➤ 37), Campanile (➤ 38), Basilica di San Marco (➤ 39), Palazzo Ducale (➤ 40), San Zaccaria (➤ 45)

❝*Don't visit Piazza San Marco on your first morning as the crowds might turn you against Venice for good. Once you've gained a taste for the city you'll be ready to venture into one of the world's most famous squares.*❞

Hordes Europe's "drawing room" was how Napoleon described Venice's main square, though glancing at its present-day summer crowds he would probably be less complimentary. The piazza is too crowded, but early in the morning or off-season its considerable charms can still work their spell. The area was initially planted with an orchard belonging to the nuns of nearby San Zaccaria. Before the building of the Basilica, Campanile, and Palazzo Ducale—the square's most famous sights—it was home to a lighthouse and a pair of churches. Its 1,000-year transformation began in the 9th century, when the nuns sacrificed their trees to make way for the Basilica and Palazzo Ducale. The 12th century saw the arrival of the Procuratie, built to house Venice's civil servants, followed in the 16th century by the Zecca (Mint) and Libreria Sansoviniana.

Sights Over and above the obvious sights and famous cafés, make a point of seeing the archaeological museum, the Torre dell'Orologio (1496–1499), complete with zodiac and 24-hour clockface, and the two granite columns that stand on the waterfront area in front of the Palazzo Ducale. One is topped with the lion of St. Mark, the other with St. Theodore and a beast of mysterious origin. The area was once a place of execution, and it is still considered unlucky to walk between the pillars. The Libreria Sansoviniana, designed by Sansovino, was considered one of the greatest buildings of its day—despite the fact that its ceiling came crashing down shortly after completion.

MUSEO CIVICO CORRER

❝*Probably only a fraction of the visitors thronging Piazza San Marco set foot in the Museo Civico Correr. Those who do not are missing not only Venice's finest museum, but also a picture gallery with a remarkable collection of paintings.*❞

History Much of the Correr's collection was accumulated by Abbot Teodoro Correr, a Venetian worthy, and left to the city in 1830. Today, it spreads over three floors, devoted respectively to historical displays, an art gallery, and the small Museo del Risorgimento (this details the 19th-century unification of Italy). The opening rooms feature lovely old prints and paintings of the city, closely followed by salons devoted to different episodes of Venetian history. Particularly outstanding are the rooms of costumes and hats, standards, armor, globes, old weapons, and ships' instruments. Perhaps the most memorable section, however, is that devoted to footwear and the famous "platform" shoes once worn by Venetian ladies of rank.

Art The last section of the second floor consists of a large hall devoted to several fine sculptures by Antonio Canova. Be sure to look for the touching study of Daedalus fixing a pair of flimsy wings to Icarus's arms. Upstairs, the third floor is devoted to the city's second-finest art gallery after the Accademia. Its most popular picture is Carpaccio's *Two Women* (1507), a masterful study of ennui that was for many years known as *The Courtesans* after its protagonists' plunging necklines. Other well-known paintings include *The Man in the Red Hat* (by either Carpaccio or Lorenzo Lotto) and a *Pietà* by Antonello da Messina, together with works by Cosmè Tura, Alvise Vivarini, and Jacopo, Giovanni and Gentile Bellini.

HIGHLIGHTS

- Aerial view of Venice (1500), Jacopo de' Barbari
- *Daedalus and Icarus*, Canova
- *Two Women*, Carpaccio
- *The Man in the Red Hat*, Lorenzo Lotto (attributed)
- *Pietà*, Antonello da Messina
- *Madonna and Child*, Giovanni Bellini

Gentile Bellini's Doge Giovanni Mocenigo

INFORMATION

- ✚ G12
- ✉ Procuratie Nuove, Ala Napoleonica, Piazza San Marco
- ☎ 522 5625
- 🕐 Wed–Mon 10–5
- 🍴 Piazza San Marco
- 🚌 San Marco 1, 3, 4, 82
- ♿ Poor
- 🎫 Expensive (joint ticket with Palazzo Ducale)
- ↔ Piazza San Marco (➤ 36), Campanile (➤ 38), Basilica di San Marco (➤ 39), Palazzo Ducale (➤ 40)

15

CAMPANILE

INFORMATION

- G12
- Piazza San Marco
- 522 4064
- Daily: Jul–Aug, 9:30–7:30. Rest of year: 9:30 to between 3:30 and 7
- Piazza San Marco
- San Marco or San Zaccaria 1, 3, 4, 52, 82
- Poor: narrow access to elevator
- Moderate
- Piazza San Marco (➤ 36), Museo Civico Correr (➤ 37), Basilica di San Marco (➤ 39), Palazzo Ducale (➤ 40), San Zaccaria (➤ 45)

One look at the lines might be enough to put you off taking the elevator up the Campanile, but you should grit your teeth and wait in line, for the views from the top—which stretch to the Alps on a clear day—are absolutely unforgettable.

Purpose Venice's tallest building (323 feet) was reputedly founded in 912 on April 25, the feast day of St. Mark. In its earliest role it served as a bell tower for the Basilica and as a lighthouse for the harbor below. Its summit was sheathed in bronze, designed to catch the sun's rays and act as a beacon during the day. Venetians had long trusted the Campanile's supposedly massive foundations, reputed to fan out in a star-shaped bulwark below the piazza. In fact, they were just 66 feet deep, a design fault exacerbated over the centuries by wind, rain, and saltwater erosion, not to mention countless lightning strikes.

Collapse Disaster struck on July 14, 1902, when, after a few warning cracks, the 990-year-old Campanile collapsed gently to the ground in front of a watching crowd. Remarkably no one was hurt, the only casualty being the keeper's cat which had returned to the evacuated tower to finish its breakfast. More remarkable still, the Basilica and Palazzo Ducale escaped virtually unscathed. Plans were immediately made to rebuild the tower *dov' era e com' era*—"where it was and how it was." The new Campanile was inaugurated on April 25, 1912, exactly 1,000 years after its predecessor—though this time 650 tons lighter and with an extra 1,000 foundation piles.

BASILICA DI SAN MARCO

❝*Don't be put off by the teeming crowds that engulf the Basilica di San Marco, as ultimately no one can fail to remain unimpressed by what is surely one of the world's greatest medieval buildings.*❞

Chapel The Basilica was begun in 832 to house the body of St. Mark, stolen from Alexandria by Venetian merchants four years earlier. For almost a thousand years it served as the doge's private "chapel" and the city's spiritual heart, accumulating the decorative fruits of a millennium to emerge as the most exotic hybrid of western and Byzantine architecture in Europe. The original building (destroyed by rioting) was replaced in 978 and again in 1094, the church from the latter date being more or less the one you see today.

Exploring Admiring the Basilica's treasures is exhausting, partly because there are so many, and partly because the almost constant crowds make exploring a fraught business. Still, the building remains overwhelmingly impressive, though you should spend a few minutes taking in some of the exterior details before plunging inside. These include the *Translation of the Body of St. Mark to the Basilica* (1260–1270) above the leftmost door, the façade's only original mosaic (the rest are later copies), and the superb Romanesque carvings (1240–1265) above the central door. Inside, you should see the famous bronze horses (probably 3rd century AD) in the Museo Marciano, the view from the Loggia dei Cavalli, the Treasury (full of antique silverware) and the magnificent Pala d'Oro, an altar screen encrusted with over 2,600 pearls, rubies, emeralds, and other precious stones.

HIGHLIGHTS

- Central door
- Façade mosaics
- Bronze horses
- View from Loggia dei Cavalli
- Rood screen
- Mosaic pavement
- Treasury
- Madonna de Nicopeia
- Pala d'Oro
- Interior mosaics

INFORMATION

- ✚ G/H12
- ✉ Piazza San Marco
- ☎ 522 5205
- 🕐 Mon–Fri 9:30–5:30, Sun 1–5:30
- 🍴 Piazza San Marco
- 🚏 San Marco or San Zaccaria 1, 3, 4, 52, 82
- ♿ Some steps; uneven floors
- 🎟 Museo Marciano: inexpensive. Treasury: inexpensive. Pala d'Oro: inexpensive
- ↔ Piazza San Marco (➤ 36), Museo Civico Correr (➤ 37), Campanile (➤ 38), Palazzo Ducale (➤ 40), San Zaccaria (➤ 45)

Rich decoration on the façade of St. Mark's

17

Palazzo Ducale

INFORMATION

- H12
- Piazzetta San Marco
- Palace: 522 4951. Guided tours: 520 4287
- Palace: daily. Apr–Oct: 9–7. Nov–Mar: 8:30–5. Guided tours: twice per morning Thu–Tue
- Piazza San Marco
- San Marco or San Zaccaria 1, 3, 4, 52, 82
- Poor: steps to upper floors
- Expensive (joint ticket with Muso Civico Correr)
- Museo Civico Correr (➤ 37), Campanile (➤ 38), Basilica di San Marco (➤ 39), San Zaccaria (➤ 45)

Bridge of Sighs

"Italy has a host of beautiful Gothic buildings, but none is quite as captivating as the Palazzo Ducale, the ornate and many-roomed seat of the doge and home to Venice's various offices of state for almost a thousand years."

History The first ducal palace, completed in 814, was a severe fortress built on one of the few clay redoubts in the lagoon. This burned down in 976, as did its successor in 1106. By 1419 the palace was in its third—and more or less final—incarnation. Three years later the great hall, or Sala del Maggior Consiglio, was completed, one of many additions made to the interior as the machinery of the state expanded. By 1550 most work had been completed, only to be undone by fires in 1574 and 1577, conflagrations that not only destroyed masterpieces by some of Venice's greatest painters, but also threatened the entire building with collapse. Restoration work continued on and off until the 1880s.

Details Outside, note the famous Ponte dei Sospiri (Bridge of Sighs), tucked down a canal at the palace's eastern end, and the fine sculptures on each of the building's three corners. Also take in the excellent carving of the pillars and capitals, and the palace's superb main doorway, the Porta della Carta (1438–1443), together with the famous little group of red porphyry knights, or tetrarchs, to its left. Beyond the courtyard and ticket office an ornate staircase leads up several flights to the beginning of the palace's set itinerary, a marked route leading from one lavishly decorated room to the next. Look for works by Tintoretto, Veronese, and other Venetian masters, in particular Tintoretto's gargantuan *Paradiso* (1588–1592), the world's largest oil painting, in the Sala del Maggior Consiglio.

18

SANTA MARIA DEI MIRACOLI

"A visitor soon gets used to being brought up short in Venice by surprises and unexpected views around almost every corner, but none quite compares with a first glimpse of the beautiful multicolored marbles of Santa Maria dei Miracoli."

Miracles The church was built to house an image of the Virgin, painted in 1409 and originally intended to be placed on the outside of a house (a common practice in Venice). Miracles (*miracoli*) began to be associated with the image in 1480, leading to a flood of votive donations which allowed the authorities to commission a church for the icon from Pietro Lombardo. One of the leading architects of his day, Lombardo, created a building that relied for its effect almost entirely on color, facing his church in a variety of honey-colored marbles, porphyry panels, and serpentine inlays (legend has it that the decorations consisted of leftover materials from the Basilica). A moat-like canal enhances the effect, providing a shimmering mirror for the multi-hued marbles.

Interior Lombardo's inspired way with marble continues in the interior, which is filled with an array of sculptures that were executed in tandem with his sons, Tullio and Antonio. The best is the carving on the two pillars that support the nuns' choir (near the entrance), on the half-figures of the balustrade fronting the raised choir, and among the exotica at the base of the choir's pillars. The striking ceiling is decorated with fifty *Saints and Prophets* (1528), the work of Pier Pennacchi. Nicolò di Pietro's *Madonna and Child*, the miraculous image for which the church was built, adorns the high altar.

HIGHLIGHTS

- Colored marbles
- Decorative inlays
- False pillars
- Bas-reliefs
- Nuns' choir
- Balustrade
- Pillar carving
- Raised choir
- *Madonna and Child,* Nicolò de Pietro
- Ceiling

Façade detail

INFORMATION

- G11
- Campo dei Miracoli
- 528 3903
- Mon–Sat 10–noon, 3–5
- Campo Santa Maria Nova
- Rialto 1, 3, 82
- Good: few steps
- Free
- Santa Maria Formosa (➤ 42), Santi Giovanni e Paolo (➤ 43)

19

SANTA MARIA FORMOSA

❝*Santa Maria Formosa's appeal rests partly on its surrounding square, Campo Santa Maria Formosa. An archetypal Venetian piazza, it's a pleasantly rambling affair, full of local color and lined with attractive cafés and palaces.*❞

Exterior This church takes its name from *una Madonna formosa*, a "buxom Madonna," which appeared to St. Magno in the 7th century and instructed him to follow a small white cloud and build a church wherever it settled. The present building, completed in 1492, was grafted onto an 11th-century Byzantine church, from which it borrowed its Greek-Cross plan, a common feature of Byzantine (and later) churches dedicated to the Virgin. The right-hand façade (1542) was paid for by the Cappello family, hence its statue of Vincenzo Cappello, a Venetian admiral. Note the carved face on the bell tower to the left, one of Venice's most famous grotesques.

Interior The church's interior is a unique blend of Renaissance decoration and ersatz Byzantine cupolas, barrel vaults, and narrow-columned screens. Of immediate interest are two paintings, the first being Bartolomeo Vivarini's *Madonna della Misericordia* (1473), a triptych in the first chapel on the right (south) side. It was financed by the church's congregation, depicted in the picture sheltering beneath the Virgin's protective cloak. The second, and more famous picture, Palma il Vecchio's *Santa Barbara* (1522–1524), used the artist's daughter as its model. Barbara was martyred by her own father, who was then struck down by lightning, a death-dealing blow from the heavens which made Barbara the patron saint of artillerymen—hence the cannon at the base of the painting and the cannonballs strewn around the chapel floor.

SANTI GIOVANNI E PAOLO

"Nowhere in Venice is there a greater collection of superb sculpture under one roof than in SS Giovanni e Paolo, a majestic Gothic church whose walls are lined with the funerary monuments of more than 20 of the city's doges."

Church SS Giovanni e Paolo, known locally as San Zanipolo, is rivaled only by Santa Maria Gloriosa dei Frari (➤ 28). Its appeal rests on a handful of superb paintings, its tremendous tombs, and on surroundings that include the magnificent façade of the adjacent Scuola Grande di San Marco and Verrocchio's great equestrian statue of Bartolomeo Colleoni (➤ 54). The church was begun in 1246 by Doge Giacomo Tiepolo, who is buried in the most ornate of the four wall tombs built into the façade. Inside, further tombs lie ranged around the walls, many by some of Venice's finest medieval sculptors. The best include the monuments to Doge Pietro Mocenigo (d. 1476) by Pietro, Tullio, and Antonio Lombardo (left of the main door), and to Doge Michele Morosini (d. 1382), on the wall to the right of the high altar.

Paintings The most outstanding of the church's paintings are Giovanni Bellini's beautiful and recently restored polyptych of *St. Vincent Ferrer* (second altar on the right) and the works in the right transept, which include *The Coronation of the Virgin*, attributed to Cima da Conegliano, and Lorenzo Lotto's wonderful *St. Antonius Pierozzi Giving Alms to the Poor* (1542).

HIGHLIGHTS

- Main portal
- Monument to Doge Pietro Mocenigo, Pietro Lombardo
- St. Vincent Ferrer (1465), Giovanni Bellini
- Cappella della Madonna della Pace
- St. Antonius Pierozzi Giving Alms to the Poor, Lorenzo Lotto
- Monument to Doge Michele Morosini
- Monument to Doge Andrea Vendramin (d. 1478)
- Monument to Doge Marco Corner (d. 1368), Nino Pisano
- Veronese ceiling paintings, Cappella del Rosario
- Monument to Doge Nicolò Marcello, Pietro Lombardo

INFORMATION

- ✚ H11
- ✉ Campo SS Giovanni e Paolo
- ☎ 523 5913
- 🕐 Daily 7:30–12:30, 3–7:30
- 🍴 Campo SS Giovanni e Paolo
- 🚤 Fondamente Nuove or Ospedale Civile 12, 13, 52
- ♿ Good: one step
- 🎟 Free
- ↔ Santa Maria dei Miracoli (➤ 41), Santa Maria Formosa (➤ 42)

Monument to Doge Pietro Mocenigo

21

SAN GIORGIO MAGGIORE

HIGHLIGHTS

- Façade (1559–1580)
- Lighthouses (1828)
- Campanile (1791)
- *Adoration of the Shepherds*, Jacopo Bassano
- *The Fall of Manna*, Tintoretto
- *The Last Supper*, Tintoretto
- *Sts. George and Stephen* (1593), bronzes by Niccolò Roccatagliata
- Choir
- View from the campanile

INFORMATION

- ✚ H14
- ✉ Campo San Giorgio, Isola di San Giorgio Maggiore
- ☎ 528 9900
- ◷ Daily 9:30–12, 2:30–5:30
- 🍴 Giudecca
- 🚢 San Giorgio 82
- ♿ Poor
- 💰 Campanile: inexpensive
- ↔ Piazza San Marco (➤ 36), Campanile (➤ 38), Basilica di San Marco (➤ 39), Palazzo Ducale (➤ 40)

"No one could complain at the superb view from the Campanile, but if asked their favorite viewpoint many Venetians would probably nominate the bell tower of San Giorgio Maggiore, a magnificent Palladian church near the Giudecca."

Classical The church's dazzling marble façade provides one of the great panoramic set pieces of the Venetian skyline. Founded in 790, the first church on the site was destroyed by an earthquake in 1223, together with an adjoining Benedictine monastery built in 982. While the monastery was rebuilt in 1443, the church had to wait until 1559 and the arrival of the great Vicenzan architect, Andrea Palladio. His design for the new church adopted many of the architectural idioms of the ancient world (notably the majestic four-columned portico) to produce one of Italy's most beautiful neoclassical buildings.

Interior The ancient world also influenced the rather sparse interior, where light is introduced by high windows, a device borrowed from the bathhouses of 3rd-century Rome. The major works of art are Jacopo Bassano's famous *Adoration of the Shepherds* (1582), located above the second altar on the right, and a pair of outstanding paintings by Tintoretto—*The Fall of Manna* (1594) and *The Last Supper* (1594)—located on the walls of the chancel. Also worth a look is the church's choir (1594–1598), tucked away behind the high altar. Few of the stalls, which depict *Scenes from the Life of St. Benedict*, have much individual delicacy, but their carving and overall effect are impressive. All else in the church pales, however, alongside the breathtaking view from the campanile, reached by an elevator at the end of the left aisle.

Choir stalls in San Giorgio Maggiore

SAN ZACCARIA

❝You'll never tire of visiting the church of San Zaccaria, a charming medley of Gothic and Renaissance architecture whose calm interior contains Giovanni Bellini's **Madonna and Child with Saints,** *one of Venice's most beautiful altarpieces.*❞

Changes San Zaccaria was founded in the 9th century, received a Romanesque veneer a century later, and was overhauled again in 1174. Rebuilding began once again in the 14th century, when the church acquired a Gothic feel, though no sooner had it been completed than another new church was begun. Old and new versions are still visible, the brick façade of the earlier church on the right, the white marble front of the latter to its left. The newer façade is one of the most important in Venice, displaying a moment of architectural transition from Gothic to Renaissance. The Gothic lower half is by Antonio Gambello, while the Renaissance upper section (added on Gambello's death in 1481) is the work of Mauro Coducci.

Interior The nave's second altar contains Giovanni Bellini's *Madonna and Child with Saints* (1505), one of Venice's most beautiful altarpieces. Across the nave in the second altar on the right lie the relics of San Zaccaria (Zachery or Zaccharias), the father of John the Baptist. The "museum" off the right aisle features two linked chapels, the first of which contains an early Tintoretto, *The Birth of John the Baptist* (above the main altar). Steps in the adjoining Cappella di San Tarasio lead down to a dank 9th-century crypt, final resting place of eight of the city's first doges. The chapel's vaults contain early Renaissance frescoes by Andrea del Castagno (1442), while the altars below feature three Gothic altarpieces by Antonio Vivarini.

HIGHLIGHTS

- Façade bas-reliefs (1440), Antonio Gambello
- Upper façade, Mauro Coducci
- *Madonna and Child with Saints*, Giovanni Bellini
- *Tomb of Alessandro Vittoria (1595)*
- Relics of San Zaccaria
- *The Birth of John the Baptist*, Tintoretto
- Crypt
- Vault frescoes, Andrea del Castagno
- Altarpieces, Antonio Vivarini and Giovanni d'Alemagna
- Predella, Paolo Veneziano

INFORMATION

- ✚ H12
- ✉ Campo di San Zaccaria
- ☎ 522 1257
- ◷ Daily 10–12, 4–6
- 🍴 Campo San Provolo
- 🚤 San Zaccaria 1, 10, 20, 52, 82
- ♿ Good
- 🎟 Church: free. Cappella di San Tarasio: inexpensive
- ↔ Piazza San Marco (➤ 36), Basilica di San Marco (➤ 39), Palazzo Ducale (➤ 40), Scuola di San Giorgio degli Schiavoni (➤ 46), San Giovanni in Bragora (➤ 47)

23

SCUOLA DI SAN GIORGIO DEGLI SCHIAVONI

HIGHLIGHTS

- Ceiling
- St. George Slaying the Dragon
- Triumph of St. George
- St. George Baptising the Gentiles
- The Miracle of St. Tryphon
- The Agony in the Garden
- The Calling of St. Matthew
- Miracle of the Lion
- The Funeral of St. Jerome
- The Vision of St. Augustine

INFORMATION

- J12
- Calle dei Furlani
- 522 8828
- Apr–Oct: Tue–Sat 9:30–12:30, 3–6:30. Nov–Mar: Tue–Sat 10–12:30, 3–6. Sun: mornings only
- Fondamenta di San Lorenzo
- San Zaccaria 1, 52, 82
- Good
- Moderate
- San Zaccaria (➤ 45), San Giovanni in Bragora (➤ 47), Museo Storico Navale (➤ 48)

"Admiring paintings in galleries is enjoyable, but to look at works of art in the buildings for which they were painted is an added bonus. This intimate scuola, with its charming cycle of Carpaccio paintings, allows you to do just that."

Slavs This tiny *scuola* was founded in 1451 to look after Venice's Dalmatian, or Slav (*Schiavoni*), population. Dalmatia, roughly present-day Croatia, was among the first territories absorbed by Venice (in the 9th century). By the 15th century the city had a large community of expatriate Dalmatian sailors, artisans, and merchants. In 1502 Carpaccio was commissioned to decorate their humble *scuola* with scenes from the lives of Dalmatia's three patron saints: George, Tryphon, and Jerome. On their completion (in 1508), the paintings were installed in the headquarters' upper gallery, only to be moved to their present position when the *scuola* was rebuilt in 1551.

Paintings Nine paintings, plus an altarpiece by Carpaccio's son, Benedetto, lie ranged around the walls under one of the loveliest ceilings imaginable. The cycle starts on the left-hand wall with *St. George Slaying the Dragon*, a wonderfully graphic painting which, like much of Carpaccio's work, is enlivened with a wealth of exotic and extraneous detail. Moving right you come to the *Triumph of St. George*, *St. George Baptising the Gentiles*, and *The Miracle of St. Tryphon*, the last depicting the obscure boy-saint exorcising a demon from the daughter of the Roman Emperor Gordian. The next two paintings, *The Agony in the Garden* and *The Calling of St. Matthew*, are followed by three works concerned with St. Jerome, of which the best known is the last: *The Vision of St. Augustine*, in which Augustine is visited by a vision announcing Jerome's death.

SAN GIOVANNI IN BRAGORA

❝*Choosing a favorite small Venetian church is no easy matter as there are so many contenders, but many lovers of the city have a soft spot for San Giovanni in Bragora, the baptismal church of the Venetian composer Antonio Vivaldi.*❞

Names Founded in the 8th century, San Giovanni in Bragora is one of Venice's oldest churches, its name deriving possibly from *brágora*, meaning "market-place"; or from two dialect words, *brago* ("mud") and *gora* ("stagnant canal"); or from the Greek *agora*, meaning "town square"; or from *bragolare* ("to fish"); or from the region in the Middle East which yielded the relics of St. John the Baptist, to whom the church is dedicated. The Venetian composer Antonio Vivaldi was baptised here, and the original font, together with copies of the baptismal documents, stands at the beginning of the left nave.

Paintings The paintings in the lovely interior begin on the right wall to the left of the first chapel with a triptych by Francesco Bissolo and a *Madonna and Saints* by Bartolomeo Vivarini. Between these, above the confessional, stands a small Byzantine Madonna. A relief above the sacristy door is flanked on the left by Alvise Vivarini's *Risen Christ* (1498) and on the right by Cima da Conegliano's *Constantine and St. Helena* (1502). Cima also painted the church's pictorial highlight, *The Baptism of Christ* (1494), its beautiful frame and ethereal blues offset by the high altar's stuccoed vaults. No less lovely are two paintings on the wall of the left aisle: a small *Head of the Saviour* by Alvise Vivarini; and Bartolomeo Vivarini's enchanting *Madonna and Child* (1478), to the right of the second chapel.

HIGHLIGHTS

- Façade
- Vivaldi's baptismal font
- *Madonna and Saints*, Bartolomeo Vivarini
- Byzantine Madonna
- Relics of St. John the Almsgiver (second chapel on right)
- *Risen Christ*, Alvise Vivarini
- *Constantine and St. Helena*, Cima da Conegliano
- *The Baptism of Christ*, Cima da Conegliano
- *Head of the Savior*, Alvise Vivarini
- *Madonna and Child*, Bartolomeo Vivarini

INFORMATION

- ✠ J12
- ✉ Campo Bandiera e Moro
- ☎ 522 9651
- 🕐 Mon–Sat 9:30–11, 3:30–5:30
- 🍴 Campo Bandiera e Moro
- 🚇 Arsenale or San Zaccaria 1
- ♿ Good
- 🎫 Free
- ↔ San Zaccaria (➤ 45), Scuola di San Giorgio degli Schiavoni (➤ 46), Museo Storico Navale (➤ 48)

Vivaldi's baptismal font

25

MUSEO STORICO NAVALE

- Manned torpedoes
- Painted galley friezes
- Gondola displays
- Models of Venetian galleys
- Model of the *Bucintoro*
- Padiglione delle Navi
- Painted fishing boats
- Funeral barge
- Arsenale gateway

Model of the Bucintoro

INFORMATION

- Museum: K13. Padiglione delle Navi: K13
- Museum: Campo San Biagio. Padiglione delle Navi: Fondamenta dell'Arsenale
- 520 0276
- Mon–Sat, 9–1
- Via Giuseppe Garibaldi
- Arsenale 1
- Poor
- Inexpensive
- Scuola di San Giorgio degli Schiavoni (➤ 46), San Giovanni in Bragora (➤ 47)

If you expected a dull and perfunctory museum, Venice's Museo Storico Navale is a revelation. Its enjoyably presented displays of maritime ephemera place Venice and the sea, its inseparable ally, into a clear historical context.

Boats The idea of a maritime museum was originated in 1815 by the Austrians, who collected remnants of the Venetian Navy (dispersed and partly destroyed by Napoleon) and mixed them with scale models of Venetian vessels and other pieces of maritime ephemera. In 1958 the collection, swollen over the years, was moved to its present site close to the entrance to the Arsenale, the great shipyards which once produced the galleys that formed the cornerstone of Venice's far-flung empire. Before or after seeing the museum, it is well worth walking the short distance north to Campo Arsenale to admire the fine Renaissance gateway (1460) which marks the entrance to the yards (now in the hands of the Italian Navy).

Museum The four-floor museum traces the history of the Venetian and Italian navies, illustrating their development with a succession of uniforms, medals, flags, pendants, maps, diagrams, cannon, mortars, machine guns, and beautifully crafted scale models of forts and boats. Look for the models of the *triremi*, the oar-driven galleys that formed the core of the Venetian fleet. Displays on the fourth floor are devoted to the gondola. The mezzanine has a shimmering collection of shells and a display on the unexpectedly close links between the maritime traditions of Venice and Sweden. Be sure to visit the separate Padiglione delle Navi, a wonderful collection of gondolas, funeral barques, and other lovely old boats housed in the Arsenale's former oarsmakers' sheds.

VENICE's *best*

PAINTINGS

The Miracle of the Cross at Ponte San Lorenzo by Gentile Bellini

GENTILE BELLINI
The Miracle of the Cross at Ponte San Lorenzo (1500)
One of a cycle of paintings depicting "The Miracles of the True Cross," this picture shows the head of the Scuola di San Giovanni Evangelista holding aloft a reliquary containing a fragment of the "True Cross" (the reliquary had accidentally been dropped into a canal and floated miraculously to the surface).
Location Gallerie dell'Accademia (➤ 31)

Family portrait

Iacopo Pesaro, who commissioned Titian's *Madonna di Ca' Pesaro*, is depicted in the painting in front of the knight on the left (who may be a self-portrait of Titian). Pesaro led a fleet against the Turks in 1502, partly in response to a call from the Borgia pope, Alexander VI—hence the knight in armor behind Pesaro, whose standard bears the Pesaro and Borgia coats of arms. The same figure leads a turbanned Turk and black slave toward St. Peter, a symbol of their conversion and of the Christian spirit of the campaign. On the right, St. Francis holds his hands over Iacopo's brother, Francesco, while the boy looking out from the painting is Iacopo's nephew and heir, Lunardo. The face of the Madonna was modeled on Titian's wife, Celia, who died soon after in childbirth.

GIOVANNI BELLINI
Madonna and Child between Sts. Nicholas, Peter, Mark and Benedict (1488)
The effect of this painting is enhanced by the perspective used to place the Madonna in her gold-lined recess, and the manner in which the frame is designed to continue the painting's perspective scheme. The picture was a gift from noblemen Pietro (Peter) Pesaro and his sons Niccolò, Marco, and Benedetto—hence the choice of saints depicted.
Location Santa Maria Gloriosa dei Frari (➤ 28)

VITTORE CARPACCIO
St. George Slaying the Dragon (1502–1508)
Note the remains of the dragon's earlier victims, depicted in grisly detail in the foreground of the painting, and the manner in which the saint's lance divides the picture into compositional "triangles." Each section has its own color and narrative preoccupation: dragon and city, St. George and Selene (the princess he has saved), the sky, and the human debris of the foreground.
Location Scuola di San Giorgio degli Schiavoni (➤ 46)

VITTORE CARPACCIO
Two Women (1507)
This picture was long thought to depict a pair of courtesans, though the distinctive hairstyles and plunging necklines of the dresses were typical of many women of the time.
Location Museo Civico Correr (➤ 37)

GIAN ANTONIO FUMIANI
The Miracles and Martyrdom of St. Pantaleone (1704)
Although not artistically distinguished, this ceiling painting impresses by its sheer scale, its 60 linked panels forming the world's largest area of painted canvas.
Location San Pantalon (➤ 53)

TINTORETTO
Paradiso (1588–1592)

At 1,500 square feet this is the world's largest single oil painting. Painted free for the state when Tintoretto was in his seventies, it depicts the regiment of the saved as described in Canto XXX of Dante's *Paradiso*.
Location Palazzo Ducale (➤ 40)

TINTORETTO
Crucifixion (1565)

Victorian critic John Ruskin wrote of this painting: "I must leave this picture to work its will on the spectator, for it is beyond all analysis and above all praise." Novelist Henry James thought: "Surely no single picture in the world contains more of human life…there is everything in it."
Location Scuola Grande di San Rocco (➤ 27)

TITIAN
Assumption (1516–1518)

This powerful painting sits above the Frari's high altar, and is designed to attract your attention from most parts of the church. It was not always highly esteemed, having been criticized as too revolutionary by the Franciscans who commissioned it, and was kept in storage until earlier this century.
Location Santa Maria Gloriosa dei Frari (➤ 28)

TITIAN
Madonna di Ca' Pesaro (1526)

Bishop Pesaro (see panel) lies buried in a tomb to the right of the painting commissioned in 1519. Note the two columns that bisect the picture and the off-center position of the Madonna, both interesting compositional devices.
Location Santa Maria Gloriosa dei Frari (➤ 28)

PAOLO VERONESE
Supper in the House of Levi (1573)

This picture was painted as a *Last Supper* for the refectory of SS Giovanni e Paolo, but after complaints from the Inquisition—who objected to its "buffoons, drunkards, Germans, dwarfs and similar indecencies"—Veronese changed its name (but not its content). Veronese himself is the figure in green, center left.
Location Gallerie dell'Accademia (➤ 31)

Carpaccio's Two Women

St. Ursula

Carpaccio's painting cycle in the Accademia tells the story of St. Ursula, daughter of the Breton King Maurus, and her proposed marriage to Hereus, son of the English King Conon. It was agreed that the ceremony would take place on two conditions: first, that Hereus wait three years, and second that he convert to Christianity and accompany Ursula on a pilgrimage to Rome. Neither demand seemed unreasonable, except that the pilgrimage was to be made in the company of "11,000 virgins," and that the whole party were eventually massacred at Cologne on their return from Rome.

Carpaccio's St. George Slaying the Dragon

CHURCHES

Gesuiti trompe-l'oeil

Archway

Not far from San Giacomo, *en route* for Santa Maria Gloriosa dei Frari, stands the Scuola Grande di San Giovanni Evangelista. Once among the city's richest *scuole*, it was responsible, among other things, for commissioning the great "Miracles of the True Cross" cycle now in the Accademia (➤ 31). Today, its buildings are mostly given over to conferences and are closed to the public.

Anyone, however, can enjoy its stunning archway, designed by Pietro Lombardo in 1481. The eagle in the lunette is the symbol of St. John (San Giovanni).

Campanile, San Francesco della Vigna

52

See also listings in the Top 25 Sights ➤ 24–48

I GESUITI

This large, dank church, built by the Jesuits in 1715, is renowned for its extraordinary marble *trompe-l'œil*, best seen in the pulpit on the left, whose solid stone is carved to resemble pelmets, tassels, and curtains. The church also boasts Titian's *Martyrdom of St. Lawrence* (first chapel on the left) and Tintoretto's *Assumption of the Virgin* (left transept).

✚ G/H10 ✉ Campo dei Gesuiti ☎ 528 6579 ◷ Daily 10–12, 4–6 🚤 Fondamente Nuove 52 ♿ Good 🎟 Free

SAN FRANCESCO DELLA VIGNA

San Francesco takes its name from a vineyard (*vigna*) left to the Franciscans here in 1253. Many alterations have been made since, not least the façade, built by Palladio between 1562 and 1572. Despite its shabby surroundings, the church has many fine tombs, marble reliefs by Pietro Lombardo, a delightful cloister, and several good paintings, the best being Antonio da Negroponte's *Madonna and Child* (1450), on the right-hand wall of the right transept.

✚ J11 ✉ Campo della Confraternità ☎ 520 6102 ◷ Daily 7–12, 5–7 🚤 San Zaccaria or Celestia 1, 52, 82 ♿ Good 🎟 Free

SAN GIACOMO DELL'ORIO

Few Venetian buildings feel as old as San Giacomo, founded in the 9th century and added to over the years to produce a pleasing architectural hybrid. The 14th-century Gothic ship's-keel ceiling is outstanding, as is the wooden Tuscan statue of the *Madonna and Child*. There are magnificent paintings in the old and new sacristies (some by Veronese), two ancient marble pillars in the nave (stolen during the Fourth Crusade), a *Crucifix* by Lorenzo Veneziano, and a high altarpiece by Lorenzo Lotto of the *Madonna and Child* (1546).

✚ E10 ✉ Campo San Giacomo dell'Orio ☎ 524 0672 ◷ Daily 7.30–12, 4.30–6.30 🚤 Riva di Biasio or San Stae 1 ♿ Good 🎟 Free

SAN GIOBBE

San Giobbe began life as a 13th-century chapel dedicated to Job (Giobbe), a figure invoked against the plague. The fine portal and its four saints (1471) are the work of Pietro Lombardo. The interior is known for the Cappella Martini, created for expatriate silk weavers from Lucca—hence the majolica work by the Tuscan

based della Robbia family. The lions in the right aisle decorate the tomb of a 17th-century French ambassador. The sacristy off the right nave has a lovely ceiling and a fine triptych by Antonio Vivarini.
🔛 D9 ⊠ Campo San Giobbe ☎ 524 1889 ⏰ Daily 9–11:30, 3:30–6 🚤 Ponte dei Tre Archi 52 ♿ Good 🎟 Free

SANTA MARIA DEL GIGLIO

This church takes its alternative name (Santa Maria Zobenigo) from the Jubanico family, who reputedly financed its building in the 9th century. Another family, the 17th-century Barbaro clan, commissioned the present façade. Its five statues represent five of the Barbaro brothers, while the martial reliefs depict fortresses that featured in the brothers' military careers. Inside, the high altar is adorned with works by Tintoretto, although the church's highlight is its lovingly displayed collection of saints' relics.
🔛 F13 ⊠ Campo Santa Maria Zobenigo ☎ 522 5739 ⏰ Daily 9–12, 3:30–6 🚤 Santa Maria del Giglio 1 ♿ Poor (steps inside church) 🎟 Free

SAN NICOLÒ DEI MENDICOLI

San Nicolò is one of Venice's oldest and most charming churches. It was built in the 12th century, and since 1966 has been restored by the Venice in Peril Fund. The interior is beautifully decorated with marbles, statues, paintings and fine gilded woodwork.
🔛 B/C12 ⊠ Campo San Nicolò ☎ 528 5952 ⏰ Mon–Sat 10–12, 4–6 🚤 San Basilio 82 ♿ Good 🎟 Free

SAN PANTALON

San Pantalon is best known for its gargantuan ceiling painting, Gian Antonio Fumiani's *The Miracles and Martyrdom of St. Pantaleone* (1704) (➤ 50). Smaller paintings include Veronese's *St. Pantaleone Healing a Boy* (1587; second chapel on the right) and the *Coronation of the Virgin* (1444) by Antonio Vivarini and Giovanni d'Alemagna (in the chapel to the left of the chancel).
🔛 D12 ⊠ Campo San Pantalon ⏰ Daily 8–11:30, 4:30–7 🚤 San Tomà 1, 82 ♿ Good 🎟 Free

SAN POLO

Founded in 837, but much altered since, the church of San Polo is renowned for Giandomenico Tiepolo's *Via Crucis*, or *Stations of the Cross* (1747), an 18-panel cycle of paintings in the sacristy. Tintoretto's turbulent *Last Supper* (1547) hangs to the sacristy's left (on the west wall), while the apse chapel to the left of the high altar contains Veronese's *Marriage of the Virgin*.
🔛 E/F11 ⊠ Campo San Polo ☎ 523 7631 ⏰ Daily 8–12, 4–6 🚤 San Silvestro 1 ♿ Good 🎟 Free

Minor churches

During your exploration of the city look for the following:

● Gesuati—richly decorated interior with a ceiling fresco by G.B. Tiepolo and paintings by Tintoretto, Piazzetta, and Sebastiano Ricci (🔛 E13).

● San Giacomo di Rialto—tiny 5th-century church, reputedly Venice's oldest, known for its Gothic portico and lovely clock (🔛 G11).

● San Moisè—boasts the most elaborate baroque façade in the city: look for the many grotesques (🔛 G12).

● San Salvatore—beautiful Renaissance interior with two paintings by Titian: *The Annunciation* (third altar on the right) and *The Transfiguration* above the high altar (🔛 G11).

● San Trovaso—contains Tintoretto's final two works (either side of the choir) and the superb *St. Chrysogonus on Horseback* (chapel right of the high altar) by Michele Giambono (🔛 E13).

San Nicolò dei Mendicoli

SQUARES

Bartolomeo Colleoni

Born in Bergamo, Colleoni, the noted 15th-century mercenary, began his military career in Naples aged 19, entering Venetian service in 1431. After spells working for Milan, he returned to the Venetian cause in 1455. Over the next 20 years, however, he was called upon to fight only once. His name is a corruption of *coglioni*, meaning "testicles," a play on words of which Colleoni was proud (*coglioni* featured conspicuously on his emblem). Thomas Coryat, an English traveller to Venice in 1611, repeated a story (put about by Colleoni himself) that "Bathelmew Coleon…had his name from having *three* stones, for the Italian word Coglione doth signifie a testicle."

Piazza San Marco

See Top 25 Sights for
PIAZZA SAN MARCO ► 36

CAMPO DEI MORI

This sleepy little square may take its name either from the Moorish merchants who traded on the *fondaco* near by, or from three silk merchants—Robia, Sandi, and Alfani Mastelli—who left the Peloponnese (Morea) in 1112 to settle in the Palazzo Mastelli north of the *campo* (recognizable by the bas-relief of a camel). In time they may have inspired the so-called *Mori* (*Moors*), three statues built into the walls of the piazza's houses. The building just east of the square at No. 3399 (with a plaque) was home to the painter Tintoretto between 1574 and his death in 1594.

➕ F9 ✉ Cannaregio 🚤 Madonna dell'Orto 52

CAMPO SS GIOVANNI E PAOLO

The church of SS Giovanni e Paolo in this square should not distract you from the statue of Bartolomeo Colleoni at its center, nor the lovely façade of the Scuola Grande di San Marco on its northern flank. The *scuola*, now a hospital, was once the wealthiest in Venice and boasted a headquarters that was rivaled only by the Scuola Grande di San Rocco (► 27). Its façade was begun in 1487 by Pietro Lombardo (responsible for many of the sculptures in the church) and completed eight years later by Mauro Coducci, an architect active in the nearby churches of Santa Maria Formosa and San Zaccaria (► 42 and 45). The statue of Colleoni (1481–1496), often called Italy's greatest equestrian sculpture, is mostly the work of the Florentine sculptor Andrea Verrocchio. Colleoni was a famous *condottiere*, or mercenary soldier (see panel), who left his vast fortune to Venice on the condition that the city erected a statue of him in Piazza San Marco. The state took his money, but was unwilling to glorify any individual in its most famous square and so slyly erected a statue in the more modest *Campo* San Marco instead.

➕ H11 ✉ Castello 🍴 Cafés 🚤 Ospedale Civile 52

CAMPO SANTA MARGHERITA

This may well become your favorite Venetian square, thanks mainly to its friendly and informal air, its collection of pleasant little bars and cafés, and its easy-going streetlife, which reminds you that Venice is still—just—a living city. Venetians meet here to chat, shop, and sip coffee while their children play raucously on the square's ancient flagstones. Causin, noted for its ice cream, is the longest established of the cafés, but Il Caffè and Il Doge are both equally fine places to sit and watch the world go by. The square is convenient to many sights, notably San Pantalon (► 53), the Scuola Grande dei Carmini (► 26), San Sebastiano (► 25), the Scuola Grande di San Rocco and Frari (► 27 and 28), the Accademia (► 31), and the Ca' Rezzonico (► 29).

🞜 D12 🖂 Dorsoduro 🍴 Cafés 🚤 Ca' Rezzonico 1

CAMPO SANTA MARIA FORMOSA

Like all of Venice's more intriguing squares, Campo Santa Maria Formosa is distinguished by an old-world Venetian atmosphere, its charm assured by a combination of market stalls, local streetlife and welcoming cafés and bars. Although only a stone's throw from Piazza San Marco, the square escapes the attention of most tourists but is convenient to several key sights, not least of which is the church of Santa Maria Formosa, whose crumbling façade dominates its southern flank (► 42).

🞜 H11 🖂 Castello 🍴 Cafés 🚤 Rialto 1, 3, 82

CAMPO SAN POLO

Campo San Polo is the largest of Venice's squares after Piazza San Marco, but sits at the heart of the smallest of the city's six *sestieri*. Once the scene of bullfights, mass sermons, and masked balls, it is now a homey setting for elderly matrons and their dogs, and groups of mothers with their children, who play soccer and ride their bikes. Informal sidewalk cafés provide a vantage point on the comings and goings, while the church of San Polo (► 53) and the Palazzo Soranzo (once home to Casanova) add a more formal note to the squaare.

🞜 E/F11 🖂 San Polo 🍴 Cafés 🚤 San Silvestro 1

CAMPO SANTO STEFANO (CAMPO FRANCESCO MOROSINI)

After Campo Santa Margherita, this is probably the most pleasant square for a break from sightseeing, and in particular from the church of Santo Stefano (► 30) and the nearby Accademia (► 31). Until 1802 it was used for bullfights, during which bulls or oxen were tied to a stake and baited by dogs. For years the area was grassy, all except for a stone avenue known as the Liston. This became such a popular place to stroll that it led to a Venetian expression *andare al 'iston*, meaning "to go for a walk." The square's nicest café is Paolin, considered by many to serve the best ce cream in the city.

🞜 F12 🖂 San Marco 🍴 Cafés 🚤 San Samuele 3, 4, 82

Campo Santa Margherita

Sior Antonio

A fourth figure complements Campo dei Mori's three famous Moorish statues. Known as Sior Antonio Rioba, and distinguished by its rusty metal nose, it peers down from the corner of a building on the east of the square. Anonymous denunciations of the state were once signed with his name and left pinned at his feet, a practice recalling "Pasqualino" in Rome, a statue at which *pasquinades* (usually papal denunciations) were left.

55

VIEWS

View from the Campanile

People-watching

The Loggia dei Cavalli is home to the famous bronze horses of the Basilica di San Marco (though today's versions are copies, the originals are kept inside the Basilica to protect them from pollution), but it also offers a tremendous view over Piazza San Marco and its swirling crowds. There are few better places in the whole of Italy to indulge in people-watching.

🚻 G/H12 🖂 Piazza San Marco ☎ 522 5205 🕐 Mon–Fri 9:30–5:30, Sun 1–5:30 🍽 Piazza San Marco 🚤 San Marco or San Zaccaria 1, 3, 4, 52, 82 🚹 Poor 🎟 Inexpensive

CAMPANILE

You will probably face lines for the Campanile (➤ 38), but the view—which extends to the Alps on a clear day—is more than worth the wait. Goethe first saw the sea from here, while Galileo used the panorama to demonstrate his telescope.

🚻 G12 🖂 Piazza San Marco ☎ 522 4064 🕐 Daily. Jul–Aug: 9:30–7.30. Rest of year: 9:30 to varying times between 3:30 and 7 🍽 Piazza San Marco 🚤 San Marco or San Zaccaria 1, 3, 4, 52, 82 🚹 Poor: narrow access to elevator 🎟 Moderate

PONTE DELL'ACCADEMIA

All the bridges across the Grand Canal (➤ 24) offer mesmerizing views, but none perhaps as pretty as those from the Ponte dell'Accademia. Below you boats and gondolas flit about, while the Grand Canal curves gently to the east and west, offering views of distant palaces and Santa Maria della Salute.

🚻 E13 🖂 Canal Grande 🕐 Always open 🚤 Accademia 1, 3, 4, 82 🚹 Poor 🎟 Free

PONTE DI RIALTO

While the Ponte dell'Accademia offers a sublime general view of the Grand Canal, the Ponte di Rialto provides an overview of a stretch that is narrow yet frantically busy. You could spend a lot of time here simply soaking in the comings and goings beneath you, or casting your eye over the people jostling for position on the Fondamenta del Vin.

🚻 G11 🖂 Canal Grande 🕐 Always open 🍽 Cafés on the Fondamenta del Vin 🚤 Rialto 1, 3, 82 🚹 Poor 🎟 Free

PUNTA DELLA DOGANA

The *sestiere* of Dorsoduro narrows to a point at the Punta della Dogana to offer a fine view across the mouth of the Grand Canal to the north (taking in the Campanile and Palazzo Ducale) and across the Canale della Giudecca to the south (with excellent views of San Giorgio Maggiore and the Giudecca).

🚻 G13 🖂 Canal Grande 🕐 Always open 🚤 Santa Maria della Salute 1 🚹 Good 🎟 Free

SAN GIORGIO MAGGIORE

The view from the bell tower of Palladio's church (➤ 44) is perhaps the best in the city, surpassing that of the Campanile by virtue of the fact that it offers a panorama which *includes* the Campanile and offers a better overview of the lagoon and the Giudecca.

🚻 H14 🖂 Campo San Giorgio, Isola di San Giorgio Maggiore ☎ 52? 9900 🕐 Daily 9:30–12, 2:30–5:30 🍽 Giudecca 🚤 San Giorgio 82 🚹 Poor 🎟 Inexpensive

FAÇADES

CA' PESARO

Like many of Venice's finest palaces, the Ca' Pesaro presents its best face to the Grand Canal, but with some judicious route-finding its waterfront façade can also be glimpsed from the ends of several alleys off the Strada Nova. It was bought as three separate buildings in 1628 by the Pesaro family, who subsequently commissioned Baldassare Longhena, one of Venice's leading 17th-century architects, to unite the component parts behind one of the city's grandest baroque façades. Today it houses Venice's Museo Orientale, a collection of Chinese and Japanese art and artefacts.

➕ F10 ✉ Canal Grande-Fondamenta Pesaro 📷 Museo Orientale: 524 1173 🎦 Museo Orientale: Tue–Sun 9–2 🚤 San Stae 1 ♿ Poor 💶 Museo Orientale: moderate

PALAZZO DARIO

The Palazzo Dario possesses perhaps the most charming façade of any Venetian palace, its appeal heightened by the building's rather alarming lean. Built in the 1480s, it was probably designed by Pietro Lombardo, whose use of inlaid colored marbles is repeated in his masterpiece, Santa Maria dei Miracoli (➤ 41). It has long been believed that the palace is cursed. It is best seen from the Grand Canal or the Santa Maria del Giglio landing stage opposite.

➕ F13 ✉ Calle Barbaro 🎦 Not open to the public 🚤 Santa Maria del Giglio 1

PALAZZO VENDRAMIN-CALERGI

The masterpiece of the Grand Canal, this palace was begun by Mauro Coducci at the end of the 15th century and finished in the first decade of the 16th century, probably by Tullio Lombardo. The composer Richard Wagner occupied a 15-room suite here during his last months. When he died in the palace in February 1883, his body was taken to the station by gondola in the dead of night for subsequent burial at Bayreuth. Today, the palace is the winter home of the Casinò Municipale. The façade is best seen from the Canal or from the Calle del Megio opposite.

➕ F10 ✉ Canal Grande-Calle Larga Vendramin 🚤 San Marcuola 1, 82

Façades

A palace's waterfront façade was the most elaborate and the only one faced with stone, which was both costlier and heavier than brick, and therefore a burden on the building's foundations (these consisted of wooden piles driven into the mud). The ground floor was marked by a gate opening onto the canal and entrance hall (*andron*), used for deliveries and access by gondola. Above, windows mark the *mezzanino*, a labyrinth of small rooms used as offices, and above them a row of larger windows which indicate the *piano nobile*, the grandest of the palace's living areas. This consisted of suites arranged around the *portego*, a broad corridor through the building that encouraged cool breezes to pass through in summer.

Façade of the Palazzo Dario

BOAT TRIPS

Vaporetto *on the Grand Canal*

Gondola rides

Hiring a gondola is enchanting but expensive. In theory, the official tariff is around L80,000 for a 50-minute ride for up to five passengers, rising to about L100,000 for the same trip between 8PM and 8AM. An extra L40,000 or so is levied for each additional 25 minutes, and more for any musical accompaniment. In practice, rates are more negotiable, so confirm the price *and* the duration of a trip before departure. Do not be afraid to walk away or haggle if the prices seem too high—there are plenty of gondoliers. Most gondoliers have a set route, so if you wish to see a particular part of the city discuss your preferences before fixing a price. Also note the location of official stands: Riva del Carbon (near the Rialto); Campo San Moisè; Santa Maria del Giglio; Bacino Orseolo (northwest of Piazza San Marco); at the train station; and the Danieli hotel.

See Top 25 Sights for CANAL GRANDE ➤ 24

ISLANDS

The No. 12 steamer from the Fondamente Nuove runs every 60–90 minutes to the islands of Burano and Torcello, a 45-minute trip that offers not only two interesting end destinations, but also provides excellent views of Venice and the Venetian lagoon. (See panel ➤ 21 for details of the *Biglietto Isole*, a special "Islands Ticket.")

🏠 H10 ✉ Fondamente Nuove 🚤 Fondamente Nuove 12 💰 Expensive

LA GIUDECCA AND THE DOCKS

Catching *vaporetto* 82 at San Zaccaria and staying on board past San Giorgio and the Giudecca to Piazzale Roma will give you not only a good view of San Giorgio Maggiore and the Giudecca ahead (and San Marco behind), but also an interesting insight into the area around the docks and Stazione Marittima, the busy and little-visited commercial port area in the southeast of the city.

🏠 H12 ✉ Riva degli Schiavoni 🚤 San Zaccaria 82 💰 Moderate

LIDO

In the late 19th century the Lido—which lies 20 minutes south of Venice by boat—was one of the most exclusive swimming establishments in Europe. This is less true today and, unless you wish to spend time on a beach during your stay, the island is best seen from the No. 1 *vaporetto*, which can be boarded at any of the stops on the Grand Canal or San Zaccaria. The service provides fine views back to San Marco and a view of enough of the Lido to satisfy most people's curiosity.

🏠 H12 ✉ Riva degli Schiavoni 🚤 San Zaccaria 1 💰 Moderate

MURANO AND ARSENALE

The Arsenale, Venice's vast former shipyards, are now occupied by the military and are out of bounds to the general public. The only way to catch a glimpse of the yards, whose boats provided the wherewithal for Venice's supremacy at sea, is to take the No. 521 boat from Tana. This is permitted to pass through a canal that bisects the yards, and has the added advantage that it continues to Murano, circles the island, and then returns to the Fondamente Nuove before proceeding around the northern shore of the city to the Canale di Cannaregio and Piazzale Roma.

🏠 K12/13 ✉ Campiello della Malvasia 🚤 Tana 521 💰 Moderate

FREE ATTRACTIONS

See Top 25 Sights for

CHURCHES
Churches rarely charge, and where they do, as in the case of the Frari (➤ 28), the entrance fee is invariably modest. Most have some artistic treasure—a sculpture, a Tintoretto, a Bellini altarpiece—which makes a visit more than worthwhile (➤ 50–51 and 52–53).

MUSIC
You may occasionally come across free organ, choral, or chamber recitals in Venetian churches. Look for posters or contact the tourist office for details. Mass is usually sung in the Basilica di San Marco at 9AM on weekdays and 10AM on Sundays and feast days. Vespers are sung at 5:30PM in winter and 6PM in summer.

PAINTINGS
Many of Venice's finest paintings can be seen for free. These include masterpieces by Veronese (➤ 25), Tintoretto (➤ 33), Titian (➤ 52), and the Bellini altarpieces of San Pietro Martire, Santi Giovanni e Paolo, and San Zaccaria (➤ 20, 43, and 45).

RIALTO MARKETS
The Rialto has it all, whether you want to shop for souvenirs, people-watch, or revel in the sights and smells of a market. Early in the morning, before the crowds arrive, is the best time for a stroll around the fantastic medley of food and fish stalls (➤ 81).

SQUARES
Venetian squares offer the chance not only to watch your fellow visitors, but also provide an opportunity to take in the Venetians at work and play. Both groups offer endless people-watching opportunities. For the price of a cup of coffee you can observe everything from the comfort of a café terrace (➤ 54–55).

STROLLING
Venice's finest free sight is Venice itself. No city in the world offers as many beautiful views, intriguing streets, and magical buildings. Almost any walk has its rewards, the more so if you stroll around early in the morning or late at night (➤ 16–18 and 56).

Parks and gardens
Venice is a city whose peculiar make-up means it has little room left over for public parks and gardens. Still, there are one or two areas of green space where you can escape the rigors of sightseeing. In the heart of the city these are restricted to the small Giardinetti Reali (⊞ G12/13) immediately south of Piazza San Marco (but entered from the waterfront). On the city's fringes are the much larger Giardini Pubblici (⊞ L14) and more modest Giardino Papadopoli (⊞ C/D11). Further afield, the islands of Burano and Torcello have extensive areas of open space (➤ 20–21).

Giardini Pubblici

ATTRACTIONS FOR CHILDREN

Restaurants

Pizzerias and more casual restaurants are usually welcoming, though special facilities such as highchairs are rarely available. If you want a small serving ask for *una mezza porzione*. Upscale restaurants on the whole will not take kindly to smaller children, though the Italians are generally far more tolerant than many northern Europeans.

Carnival masks

BOAT TRIPS
Children should be captivated by the things to see from Venice's *vaporetti* and *motoscafi*. The best short trip is along the Grand Canal (► 24), while the best longer ride (on a larger boat) is out to the islands of Burano, Murano, and Torcello (► 20–21).

GLASS-BLOWING
Many of the glass workshops and showrooms on Murano (► 20) offer the chance to watch glass-blowers in action (glass-blowers can usually be encouraged to make a small glass gift for children).

GONDOLAS
Gondolas are large enough to accommodate at least two adults and two children, and are rented by time rather than the number of passengers. See panel (► 58) for details of prices and how to hire gondolas. Note that Grand Canal rides can be choppy.

ICE CREAM
Italian ice cream should satisfy the most demanding of young palates. Some of Venice's best *gelato* is to be found at Paolin in Campo Santo Stefano (Campo Francesco Morosini), Causin and Il Doge in Campo Santa Margherita, and Nico on the Zattere ai Gesuati (► 74–75 for more details).

LIDO
The Lido offers the chance to swim or play on the beach, as well as the excitement of the boat trip from Venice (take *vaporetto* No. 1). It is also possible to rent bikes and pedal boats at several outlets along the promenade. Note that many of the Lido's beaches are owned by hotels; public beaches (*spiaggia* or *zona comunale*) are clearly marked.

MARKETS
The strange sights, sounds, and smells of the Rialto markets (► 81) are memorable, although the more bizarre and bloody seafood of the Pescheria (fish market) may upset youngers.

MASKS
Children might enjoy buying and wearing Venice's famous masks, or simply window-shopping among the city's better-known mask shops (► 78–79).

MUSEUMS
Of Venice's museums the Museo Storico Navale (► 48) is best of all for children, while the Museo Civico Courer (► 37) also offers interest, although some bits may be a little too dusty or arty.

VENICE
where to...

LUXURY HOTELS

Tight squeeze

Venice has been accommodating visitors for hundreds of years, although over the last couple of decades the sheer number of tourists to the city has strained its 200 or so hotels to capacity, and brought about a slide in standards among the more cynical hoteliers (who know they are guaranteed customers however grim their hotels). Prices are also higher than in most of Italy (see panel opposite), and reservations are now a virtual necessity all year round (see panel ➤ 64). Noise, location, and actually finding a room are other important accommodation considerations (see panels ➤ 65–67).

CIPRIANI

Venice's most expensive hotel is a relative newcomer having opened in 1963, but has quickly become a byword for luxury and decadence. Facilities include a Jacuzzi in every suite, an Olympic-sized swimming-pool, butler service, and a renowned restaurant. The hotel occupies gardens on the eastern end of the Giudecca, with the result that you can feel slightly isolated from the sights and action of the city proper.
🞢 H14 ✉ Giudecca 10 ☎ 520 7744; fax 520 3930 🚢 Zitelle 52 ❓ Private launch service

DANIELI

The Danieli ranks, by almost common consent, as the finest of Venice's luxury hotels—but if you stay you should make sure your room is in the old wing of the Gothic *palazzo* rather than the newer annex built in 1948. The Danieli is the choice of visiting royalty, politicians, and other VIPs.
🞢 H12 ✉ Riva degli Schiavoni-Calle delle Rasse, Castello 4196 ☎ 522 6480; fax 520 0208 🚢 San Zaccaria 1, 4, 52, 82

EUROPA E REGINA

Venice's "Big Three"—the Gritti, Cipriani, and Danieli—tend to overshadow this five-star CIGA-owned hotel, but its prices are some of the most reasonable of the city's luxury hotels. Most of its 192 rooms are

spacious and many enjoy wonderful views over a courtyard garden or across the Grand Canal, while the restaurant's canal terrace and garden are wonderfully evocative places to dine.
🞢 G13 ✉ Calle Larga (Viale) XXII Marzo, San Marco 2159 ☎ 520 0477; fax 523 1533 🚢 San Marco or Santa Maria del Giglio 1, 3, 4, 82

GRITTI PALACE

Not the most expensive hotel in Venice, but—along with the Danieli—the one traditionally considered to have the most class and *élan*. Housed in a 15th-century *palazzo* close to the Grand Canal, its 93 rooms and reception areas are all impeccably grand and old-world, as is the service. A private launch and access to a private beach are both available.
🞢 F13 ✉ Santa Maria del Giglio, San Marco 2467 ☎ 794 611; fax 520 0942 🚢 Santa Maria del Giglio 1

MONACO AND GRAND CANAL

Not as famous as other hotels in its class, but almost as stylish and elegant. As its name suggests, it overlooks the Grand Canal, and the nicest of its 74 rooms enjoy views across to Santa Maria della Salute. The hotel's restaurant has an excellent reputation.
🞢 G13 ✉ Calle Vallaresso, San Marco 1325 ☎ 520 0211; fax 520 0501 🚢 San Marco 1, 3, 4, 82

EXPENSIVE HOTELS

ACCADEMIA-VILA MARAVEGE

A 17th-century *palazzo* located just west of the Accademia which once housed the Russian Embassy. Its popular 27 rooms are still grand and are furnished with antiques, although some are rather small. There is also a garden with a view of the Grand Canal. Book well in advance.

➕ E13 ✉ Fondamenta Bollani, Dorsoduro 1058 ☎ 521 0188; fax 523 9152 🚤 Accademia 1, 3, 4, 82

CAVALLETTO E DOGE

This 96-room hotel just north of Piazza San Marco has been in business for over 200 years and has a good restaurant. Rooms are light and airy.

➕ G12 ✉ Calle Cavalletto, San Marco 1107 ☎ 520 0955; fax 523 8184 🚤 San Marco 1, 3, 4, 82

GIORGIONE

This large 70-room hotel has modern facilities and as such is one of the best in the category.

➕ G10 ✉ Campo SS Apostoli, Cannaregio 4587 ☎ 522 5810; fax 523 9092 🚤 Ca' d'Oro 1

METROPOLE

A hotel with 73 rooms on the busy waterfront by the church of the Pietà and close to Piazza San Marco. The hotel is elegant and sophisticated, with many charming old-world touches. Some rooms have broad views over the lagoon.

➕ J12 ✉ Riva degli Schiavoni ☎ 520 5044; fax 522 3679 🚤 San Marco 1, 3, 4, 82

SAN MOISÈ

The 16 rooms in this tranquil but centrally located hotel vary in size, but are all furnished in traditional old-world style.

➕ F12 ✉ Piscina San Moisè, San Marco 2058 ☎ 520 3755; fax 521 0670 🚤 San Marco or Santa Maria del Giglio 1, 3, 4, 82

SATURNIA & INTERNAZIONALE

The 95 rooms of this hotel all differ slightly, the best of them looking on to the courtyard garden. Has a romantic, old-fashioned atmosphere.

➕ F12/13 ✉ Calle Larga (Viale) XXII Marzo, San Marco 2398 ☎ 520 8377; fax 520 7131 🚤 Santa Maria del Giglio 1

SCANDINAVIA

There is considerable variety in the 27 rooms of this three-star hotel, but all are comfortable and spacious. A good location on one of Venice's nicest squares.

➕ H11 ✉ Campo Santa Maria Formosa, Castello 5240 ☎ 522 3507; fax 523 5232 🚤 Rialto 1, 3, 82

STURION

The best of this welcoming hotel's 11 rooms—which vary in price—look over the Grand Canal. Book well in advance.

➕ F11 ✉ Calle del Storione, San Polo 679 ☎ 523 6243; fax 522 8378 🚤 San Silvestro 1

Prices

Italy's hotels, including those in Venice, are classified into five categories, from one star (basic) to five stars (luxury). The prices of individual rooms should be displayed in the lobby and in the room itself. Prices for different rooms often vary within a hotel, so if a room is too expensive be sure to ask if a less pricey one is available (you may well be shown the most expensive room first). Watch out for supplements for breakfast, which may be charged even if you do not take it, and in peak periods remember that hotels may insist that you take half- or full board.

MID-RANGE HOTELS

Reservations

It is now almost essential to reserve a room in Venice for July and August, and wise to do so during the rest of the high season, which officially runs from March 15 to November 15 and from December 21 to January 6, and now in effect includes the period of Carnevale in February. Many hotels do not recognize a low season, however, and lower category hotels where you might have been able to negotiate cheaper off-season rates often close during the winter. Some hotels accept credit-card reservations over the phone, but it is always best (having phoned or faxed first) to send a firm deposit in the shape of an International Money Order. Follow this up with a confirmation of receipt and another call or fax a few days before departure to confirm your booking. ♪

AGLI ALBORETTI

This 25-room hotel was added to the fine restaurant downstairs. It is attractively located on a tree-lined street and convenient for the Accademia and Zattere. Rooms are modern and stylish, if a little small, and there is a pleasant garden. Extremely popular, especially with US and UK visitors, so be sure to reserve well in advance.

✚ E13 ✉ Rio Terrà Sant'Agnese-Antonio Foscarini, Dorsoduro 884 ☎ 523 0058; fax 521 0158 ⛴ Accademia or Zattere 1, 3, 4, 52, 82

AMERICAN

A 29-room hotel just two minutes' walk from the Accademia, but on a small canal away from the crowds. The rooms have been renovated and range in price and quality.

✚ E13 ✉ Fondamenta Bragadin, Rio di San Vio, Dorsoduro 628 ☎ 520 4733; fax 520 4048 ⛴ Accademia 1, 3, 4, 82

BOSTON

This 42-room hotel stands on one of Venice's main shopping streets and is within easy reach of Piazza San Marco. The rooms vary in terms of their furnishings and views.

✚ G12 ✉ Calle dei Fabbri, San Marco 848 ☎ 528 7665; fax 522 6628 ⛴ Rialto or San Marco 1, 3, 4, 82

CASANOVA

This comfortable hotel is located at the heart of the shopping district close to Piazza San Marco.

✚ G12 ✉ Frezzeria, San Marco 1284 ☎ 520 6855; fax 520 6413 ⛴ San Marco 1, 3, 4, 82

CLUB CRISTAL

A pleasant bed and breakfast in a quiet street near the Campo dei Gesuiti, with a pretty roof terrace for evening meals on request. There are only five double bedrooms, so be sure to book early.

✚ G10 ✉ Calle Zanardi, Cannaregio 4133 ☎ 523 7194; fax 521 2705 ⛴ Ca' d'Oro

DO POZZI

This quiet hotel has 35 rooms and is located in a pleasant courtyard square off Calle Larga (Viale) XXII Marzo close to Piazza San Marco.

✚ F/G13 ✉ Corte dei Due Pozzi, San Marco 2373 ☎ 520 7855; fax 522 9413 ⛴ Santa Maria del Giglio or San Marco 1, 3, 4, 82

FALIER

A small, well-presented hotel in a part of town that's rarely frequented, but is still convenient for the area around Santa Maria Gloriosa dei Frari and the Scuola Grande di San Rocco. Some of the 19 rooms (13 of which have private bathrooms) are somewhat small, but all are elegant and tidy, and prices are very reasonable.

✚ D11 ✉ Salizzada San Pantalon, Santa Croce 130 ☎ 710 882; fax 520 6554 ⛴ Ferrovia or San Tomà 1, 3, 4, 52, 82

FLORA

This 43-room hotel has gained a well-deserved reputation, thanks mainly to its pleasant garden. Some of the rooms, however, are rather small for the price. Located just off Calle Larga (Viale) XXII Marzo to the west of Piazza San Marco.

➕ F13 ✉ Calle Bergamaschi, San Marco 2283a ☎ 520 5844; fax 522 8217 🚤 Santa Maria del Giglio 1

KETTE

Has a quiet location just southeast of La Fenice opera house. Some of the 44 rooms are small for the price, but the rates can be very reasonable off-season.

➕ F12 ✉ Piscina San Moisè, San Marco 2053 ☎ 520 7766; fax 522 8976 🚤 San Marco or Santa Maria del Giglio 1, 3, 4, 82

LA CALCINA

The waterfront location of this 37-room hotel—best known as the house where the Victorian artist and writer John Ruskin spent much of his Venetian sojourn—and the nearby Pensione Seguso (see below) may not be to all tastes, but you are well away from the bustle of central Venice and in an interesting area of the city.

➕ E13/14 ✉ Fondamenta Zattere ai Gesuati, Dorsoduro 780 ☎ 520 6466; fax 522 7045 🚤 Zattere 52, 82

LA FENICE ET DES ARTISTES

This pleasant hotel (once the home of painter Lorenzo Lotto) has 65 rooms, so there is a good chance of finding space.

➕ F12 ✉ Campiello Fenice, San Marco 1936 ☎ 523 2333; fax 520 3721 🚤 Santa Maria del Giglio 1

PENSIONE SEGUSO

A better choice, on balance, than the nearby Calcina (see above), almost all of its 36 traditionally furnished rooms being blessed with views across either the Giudecca or San Vio canals.

➕ E13/14 ✉ Fondamenta Zattere ai Gesuati, Dorsoduro 779 ☎ 528 6858; fax 522 2340 🚤 Zattere 52, 82

SAN CASSIANO-CA' FAVRETTO

This lovely hotel is full of atmosphere, occupying a converted 14th-century *palazzo* on the Grand Canal almost opposite the Ca' d'Oro. Only half the rooms face the Grand Canal, however, the remainder looking down on to a side canal.

➕ F10 ✉ Calle della Rosa, Santa Croce 2232 ☎ 524 1768; fax 721 033 🚤 San Stae 1

SANTA MARINA

This comfortable 20-room hotel is one of Venice's newest, opened in 1990 (the annexe is even newer). It lies off the tourist trail, but is still extremely convenient for shopping and all the major sights.

➕ H11 ✉ Campo di Santa Marina, Castello 6068 ☎ 523 9202; fax 520 0907 🚤 Rialto 1, 3, 82

Noise

Although Venice is remarkably quiet, it still has its fair share of nocturnal traffic—even without cars. Churchbells clatter through the night and pedestrian chatter in the main alleys and streets is amplified in the close quarters. Traffic on the main canals can also be surprisingly noisy, and refuse boats, *vaporetti*, and food suppliers start up very early. This can put a different complexion on that apparently desirable room overlooking the Grand Canal.

BUDGET HOTELS

Location

Venice's best hotels line the Grand Canal near San Marco; the least expensive lie in the slightly grubby streets around the station and Lista di Spagna. Other concentrations of hotels are near the Rialto and in Dorsoduro, the latter being one of the city's less touristy locations. You will find the odd hotel in quiet backstreets, but there is no such thing as the "undiscovered gem." In a city as compact as Venice, however, even "poor" hotels are rarely far from the sights. Be certain when making reservations to find the hotel's exact location—street name as well as number—and remember that you may well need to carry your luggage some distance.

AI DO MORI

An 11 room hotel with just three bathrooms. Prices vary for different rooms: the best have views over the Basilica di San Marco and the Torre dell' Orologio. Friendly owners.

✚ G/H12 ✉ Calle Larga San Marco, San Marco 658 ☎ 520 4817; fax 520 5328 🚤 San Marco or San Zaccaria 1, 3, 4, 52, 82

ALEX

This hotel's excellent location near Santa Maria Gloriosa dei Frari and the Scuola Grande di San Rocco makes up for the slightly tired and dated rooms.

✚ E11 ✉ Rio Terrà Frari, San Polo 2606 ☎ 523 1341; fax 523 1341 🚤 San Tomà 1, 82

ANTICO CAPON

Seven simple rooms (six with bathroom) above a good pizzeria-restaurant (➤ 72) on one of Venice's most informal squares. Amiable owners.

✚ D12 ✉ Campo Santa Margherita, Dorsoduro 3004/b ☎ 528 5292; fax 528 5292 🚤 San Tomà or Ca' Rezzonico 1, 82

CA' FOSCARI

This relaxed and well-appointed hotel has ten rooms (none with private bathroom) and is hidden away in a little alley just south of San Tomà and Santa Maria Gloriosa dei Frari.

✚ E12 ✉ Calle della Frescada, Dorsoduro 3888 ☎ and fax 710 817 🚤 San Tomà or Ca' Rezzonico 1, 82

CANADA

This immaculate hotel has several single rooms. The best room (a double) has its own roof terrace, but you need to reserve it well in advance. Conveniently situated at the heart of the city between the Rialto and Campo Santa Maria Formosa.

✚ G11 ✉ Campo San Lio, Castello 5659 ☎ 522 9912; fax 523 5852 🚤 Rialto 1, 3, 82

DA BRUNO

An excellent location close to the Rialto outweighs the hotel's drawback of small rooms.

✚ G/H11 ✉ Salizzada San Lio, Castello 5726/a ☎ 523 0452; fax 522 1157 🚤 Rialto 1, 3, 82

DA PINO

Located just east of San Pantalon on a bustling little shopping street, this 16-room hotel has been renovated, pushing up its once bargain prices. Ideally placed for the Accademia, Santa Maria Gloriosa dei Frari, the Scuola Grande di San Rocco, and attractive squares such as Campo San Polo and Campo Santa Margherita.

✚ D12 ✉ Crosera San Pantalon, Dorsoduro 3942 ☎ 522 3646; fax 718 683 🚤 San Tomà 1, 82

DONI

An intimate hotel situated away from busy Piazza San Marco but still in a convenient and attractive location between the Basilica and San Zaccaria.

It has 13 rooms (none with private bathroom), the best of which overlook the Riva del Vin.

✚ H12 ✉ Fondamenta del Vin, off Salizzada San Provolo, Castello 4656 ☎ and fax 522 4267 🚤 San Zaccaria 1, 3, 4, 52, 82

FIORITA
Very pretty, friendly, and popular little hotel in a quaint square immediately north of Santo Stefano. There are only ten rooms (eight with private bathroom).

✚ F12 ✉ Campiello Nuovo, San Marco 3457 ☎ 523 4754; fax 522 8043 🚤 Accademia or Sant'Angelo 1, 3, 4, 82

MESSNER
Located in a quiet corner of Dorsoduro, this hotel is very handy for both the church of Santa Maria della Salute and Collezione Peggy Guggenheim. It has a lovely garden and 35 large modern rooms. However, do try to stay in the main hotel rather than the nearby annex or *dipendenza*.

✚ F13 ✉ Rio Terrà del Spezier, Dorsoduro 216 ☎ 522 7443; fax 522 7266 🚤 Santa Maria della Salute 1

MONTIN
Much of this hotel's fame derives from the well-known and expensive restaurant of the same name downstairs, although the nine rooms (none with private bathroom) are perfectly pleasant in their own right.

✚ D13 ✉ Fondamenta di Borgo, Dorsoduro 1147 ☎ 522

7151; fax 520 0255 🚤 Ca' Rezzonico or Accademia 1, 3, 4, 82

REMEDIO
This hotel has 12 rooms and is located on a tranquil side-street. Excellent central setting just 100 yards from Piazza San Marco. The furniture and fittings are simple, but the hotel is clean and the staff welcoming. The least expensive rooms have shared bathrooms.

✚ H12 ✉ Calle del Rimedio, Castello 4412 ☎ 520 6232; fax 521 0485 🚤 San Marco 1, 3, 4, 82

SAN SAMUELE
Some of the ten rooms here are pretty basic, but the general quality is much better than in many in this price range. Excellently located just north of Santo Stefano, with a welcoming owner.

✚ E12 ✉ Salizzada San Samuele, San Marco 3358 ☎ and fax 522 8045 🚤 Sant'Angelo 1

SILVA
This friendly 25-room hotel (with nine bathrooms) is just north of Piazza San Marco between San Zaccaria and Santa Maria Formosa on one of Venice's most attractive waterways.

✚ H12 ✉ Fondamenta del Rimedio, Castello 4423 ☎ 522 7643; fax 528 6817 🚤 San Zaccaria 1, 3, 4, 52, 82

Finding a room

By far the best thing to do is to plan ahead and book a room in advance (see panel ➤ 64). If you arrive in Venice without accommodations do not accept rooms from touts at the station unless you are desperate: most work for generally less salubrious hotels nearby. If you are tempted, ignore their inevitably warm reassurances and find out exactly where the hotel is located, how much the room will cost, whether it has a private bathroom, and whether the cost of breakfast is additional. Otherwise, join the lines for rooms at the tourist offices at the train station, Tronchetto, the Autorimessa car park in Piazzale Roma, at Marco Polo Airport, or at the Mestre-Marghera exit of the A4 expressway. In desperation, you could take a train to Padua (30 minutes). Unless you are unable to find a room in the right price bracket in Venice, do not stay in Mestre, the ugly and largely industrial town on the mainland.

EXPENSIVE RESTAURANTS

Harry's Bar

This famous bar and restaurant was founded in 1931 when, according to legend, a now-forgotten American ("Harry") remarked to hotel barman Giuseppe Cipriani that Venice lacked for nothing except a good bar. The enterprising Cipriani duly sought financial backing, found an old rope store near Piazza San Marco, and Harry's Bar was born. It is now a place of high prices, good food, and great cocktails, and—in the words of writer Gore Vidal—"a babble of barbaric voices…the only place for Americans in acute distress to go for comfort and advice…"

ANTICA MONTIN

This venerable restaurant has been famous for several decades and is popular with the rich and famous, although today it depends somewhat on its former reputation. The quality of food no longer justifies the high prices, but it is still an evocative place to eat, especially if you get a garden table.

✚ D13 ✉ Fondamenta di Borgo, Dorsoduro 1147 ☎ 522 7151 ⏰ Closed Tue evening, Wed ⛴ Zattere or Ca' Rezzonico 1, 52, 82

ANTICO MARTINI

The Martini was established in the 18th century, and has long been one of the most stylish of the city's restaurants. Today, classic Venetian cuisine appears on the menu, with seafood playing a key role. The stylish terrace overlooks the La Fenice opera house (recently damaged by fire) and the wine list boasts 300 labels. Meals are served until 1AM, much later than most. Very expensive.

✚ F12 ✉ Campo San Fantin, San Marco 1983 ☎ 522 4121 ⏰ Closed Tue, Wed lunchtime; dinner only Dec–mid-Mar ⛴ Santa Maria del Giglio 1

DA FIORE

This highly acclaimed restaurant produces excellent Venetian cuisine, cooked up by self-taught owners Mara and Maurizio. Since appearing as one of the "world's best" restaurants in an American publication, however, it has also become extremely difficult to secure a table. Reserve a table well in advance, and study the map before you head off as it is hard to find.

✚ E11 ✉ Calle del Scaleter, San Polo 2202 ☎ 721 308 ⏰ Closed Sun, Mon ⛴ San Stae or San Silvestro 1

DA FRANZ

One of the best seafood restaurants in Venice, despite its unfashionable peripheral location on the eastern fringe of the city (close to the Giardini Publicci). Has a terrace for alfresco dining.

✚ L13 ✉ Fondamenta San Giuseppe, Castello 754 ☎ 522 0861 ⏰ Closed Tue ⛴ Giardini 1, 52, 82

DANIELI TERRACE

Venice's upscale hotels have restaurants to match: both the Gritti and Danieli (➤ 62) have superb terraces overlooking the Grand Canal. Although the Danieli wins slightly on style and panache, both offer refined Venetian and international cooking, high prices, fine service and excellent wine lists.

✚ H12 ✉ Riva degli Schiavoni-Calle delle Rasse, Castello 4196 ☎ 522 6480 ⛴ San Zaccaria 1, 4, 52, 82

DO FORNI

This slightly self-conscious restaurant is known as one of *the* places to eat among locals and tourists alike. There are two main dining rooms, one furnished rustically and the other fashioned after an opulent *Orient*

Express cabin. Both the number of tables and menu have grown with the restaurant's success, but despite its chaotic atmosphere the food does remain good—although at a rather inflated price.

➕ G12 ✉ Calle dei Specchieri, San Marco 468 ☎ 523 2148 🚤 San Marco 1, 3, 4, 82

HARRY'S BAR

This legendary establishment is best known for its celebrity status. There is a restaurant upstairs that serves reliable fare (although it can be very good, many say it is not what it used to be), while snacks can be ordered at the downstairs bar. This is also the place to come for cocktails (dress up)—the Bellini was invented here.

➕ G13 ✉ Calle Vallaresso, San Marco 1323 ☎ 528 5777 🚤 San Marco 1, 3, 4, 82

HARRY'S DOLCI

What began as a glorified cake- and coffee-shop offshoot of Harry's Bar (see above) has turned into a restaurant every bit as good (and almost as expensive) as its parent. The refined food is Venetian, while the atmosphere is chic without being at all intimidating.

➕ D14 ✉ Fondamenta San Biagio, Giudecca 773 ☎ 522 4844 ⏰ Apr–Oct: daily, 10:30AM–3PM, 7:30–10:30PM. Nov–Mar: closed Tue 🚤 Sant'Eufemia 52, 82

LA CARAVELLA

The interior of this restaurant, one of two in the Saturnia hotel (➤ 63), has been decked out in the manner of a Venetian galley, though the over-the-top décor fails to detract from the quality of the food, which has been described by many as the best in the city. The cooking has international as well as Venetian touches. Very expensive.

➕ F13 ✉ Calle Larga (Viale) XXII Marzo, San Marco 2398 ☎ 520 8901 🚤 Santa Maria del Giglio 1

LOCANDA CIPRIANI

The wonderful setting—facing the island's two churches—and top-quality food make up for the hefty prices and somewhat pretentious décor. The garden setting is also outstanding.

➕ Off map ✉ Fondamenta dei Borgononi-Piazza Santa Fosca 29, Torcello ☎ 730 757 ⏰ Closed Tue and Jan–Feb 🚤 Torcello 12, 14

POSTE VECIE

Ingredients could hardly be fresher than at this noted and appealing fish restaurant, located in an old post house alongside the Rialto's Pescheria fish market. It offers excellent and refined cooking, along with a good wine list. The Poste Vecie is also one of the oldest restaurants in Venice, and is reputed to have been founded in 1500.

➕ F10/11 ✉ Campo della Pescaria, San Polo 1608 ☎ 721 822 ⏰ Closed Tue 🚤 Rialto 1, 3, 82

Wines

Most of Venice's wine comes from the Veneto region on the mainland. Its best-known wines are the usually unexceptional Soave (white), and Valpolicella and Bardolino (reds). More interesting whites include Soave Classico, Bianco di Custoza, Tocai, Pinot Grigio and the wines of the Bregganze region. The best white of all is Prosecco, a delicious dry sparkling wine often drunk as an aperitif. Interesting reds include Raboso, the wines of the Colle Berici and Lison-Pramaggiore regions, and two excellent dessert wines: Amarone and Recioto della Valpolicella.

MID-RANGE RESTAURANTS

First courses

Venice's best-known first courses are *sarde in saôr* (sardines in a cold onion and vinegar marinade) or a simple mixed plate of seafood (*antipasto di mare*). *Prosciutto San Daniele* is the region's best ham. Pasta is available, usually with seafood— try *spaghetti alle vongole* (pasta with clams)—but most locals prefer rice, notably *risi e bisi* (rice, peas and ham) or risotto with seafood (*risotto di mare* or *dei pescatori*), mushrooms (*funghi*), vegetables, chicken and ham (*alla sbirraglia*), or flavored with cuttlefish ink (*risotto in nero*). Tripe, snails, and quail may also feature. Fish soup (*brodetto* or *zuppa di mare*) is another popular first course, as is pasta and bean soup (*pasta e fasioli*).

AGLI ALBORETTI
Conveniently located for the Accademia, which is just two minutes' walk away, this restaurant takes its name from the trees (*alberi*) outside. It is pretty inside and out, and in summer you can eat in a pergola-shaded courtyard.
🚩 E13 ⊠ Rio Terrà Antonio Foscarini-Sant'Agnese, Dorsoduro 882 ☎ 523 0058 ⏰ Closed lunchtimes and Wed 🚤 Accademia 1, 3, 4, 82

AI MERCANTI
Ai Mercanti is situated close to the Rialto's fish market, a perfect location for a restaurant which is devoted mainly to fish and seafood. Tastefully and elegantly decorated, it makes a good alternative if the better-known Alla Madonna (see below) is full. Dishes include *risotto alle vongole, spaghetti con melanzane e calamaretti* and any number of delicious homemade desserts.
🚩 F10/11 ⊠ Campo della Pescaria, San Polo 1588 ☎ 524 0282 ⏰ Closed Sun, Mon lunchtime and 1–15 Aug 🚤 Rialto 1, 3, 82

AL CONTE PESCAOR
A tiny and high-quality fish restaurant which, despite being close to Piazza San Marco, caters mainly to Venetians.
🚩 G12 ⊠ Piscina San Zulian, San Marco 544 ☎ 522 1483 ⏰ Closed Sun during winter 🚤 San Marco 1, 3, 4, 82

AL COVO
This charming restaurant has a calm, romantic and tasteful setting with lots of flowers and candles, while in summer it is usually possible to eat out in the adjacent little square. The service is generally warm and polite, while the highly accomplished cooking focuses on traditional Venetian recipes using high-quality ingredients. Fish dishes are well to the fore, and the wine list is also good. The restaurant provides an excellent alternative to the nearby and better-known Corte Sconta (see below).
🚩 J12 ⊠ Campiello della Pescaria, Castello 3968 ☎ 522 3812 ⏰ Closed Wed, Thu and two weeks in Aug and Jan 🚤 Arsenale 1

ALLA MADONNA
This is one of Venice's most traditional restaurants, both from the point of view of food and atmosphere, encapsulating the look and feel of a Venetian restaurant of 20 or 30 years ago (it is one of the oldest in the city). It is a popular favorite for business meetings and Venetian families celebrating a special occasion. The food is good and rigorously Venetian, and includes such typical dishes as *sarde in saôr, zuppa di pesce*, and *ai frutte di mare*. The dining area is roomy and efficiently run, although with 600–700 meals served a day the service may be a little too brusque for some.
🚩 F11 ⊠ Calle della Madonna, San Polo 594 ☎ 523 3824 ⏰ Closed Wed and two weeks in Aug 🚤 Rialto 1, 3, 82

CORTE SCONTA
Many Venetians and visitors alike rate the Corte Sconta as their favorite among the city's restaurants, despite its slightly peripheral location (close to the Arsenale). It is fairly small (just 60 seats) and is always busy with tourists, despite being somewhat difficult to find—so reservations are essential. Despite its popularity, the atmosphere remains pleasant, while the cooking and seafood are rarely less than excellent. However, prices for a full meal have crept up slightly of late. In summer there is a small garden for outdoor eating.
➕ J12 ✉ Calle del Pestrin, Castello 3886 ☎ 522 7024
🕐 Closed Sun and Mon
🚤 Arsenale 1

DA ARTURO
Known in Venice for the fact that it is virtually the only top-quality restaurant in the city that concentrates on meat dishes at the expense of fish. Good wine list and a pleasant wood-paneled dining room.
➕ F12 ✉ Rio Terrà degli Assassini, San Marco 3656 ☎ 528 6974 🕐 Closed Sun
🚤 Sant'Angelo 1

DA IGNAZIO
This fish restaurant lies just east of Campo San Tomà, and has a traditional atmosphere and a garden for alfresco dining.
➕ E11 ✉ Calle Saoneri, San Polo 2749 ☎ 523 4852
🕐 Closed Sat 🚤 San Tomà 1, 82

DA REMIGIO
Old-fashioned neighborhood trattorias are a dying breed in Venice, so this authentic little local restaurant is therefore something of a rarity. It has just 40 seats, so you will definitely need to reserve or arrive early to share a table with its many satisfied customers. The food is reliable and homey, and the wine list short and to the point.
➕ J12 ✉ Salizzada dei Greci, Castello 3416 ☎ 523 0089
🕐 Closed Mon evening and Tue 🚤 San Zaccaria or Arsenale 1, 4, 52, 82

FIASCHETTERIA TOSCANA
Established in 1956, this restaurant has quite rightly been popular since it opened its doors. Despite the "Toscana" in its name, its menu includes classic Venetian dishes and seafood. Excellent selection of wines.
➕ G11 ✉ Salizzada San Giovanni Cristostomo, Cannaregio 5719 ☎ 528 5281 🕐 Closed Tue and three weeks in Jul
🚤 Rialto 1, 3, 82

FIORE
This thoroughly local trattoria has lots of color, with a popular bar serving snacks as well as an intimate restaurant. Do not confuse it with Da Fiore in San Polo (▶ 68). Located just off Campo Santo Stefano (Campo Francesco Morosini); reservations are essential.
➕ F12 ✉ Calle delle Botteghe, San Marco 3460 ☎ 523 5310
🕐 Closed Tue 🚤 San Samuele 1

Entrées

Venice's most famous entrée is calf's liver and onions (*fegato alla veneziana*), although fish and seafood form the city's main culinary staples. Mussels (*cozze* or *peoci)* from the lagoon are common, together with cuttlefish (*seppie*) and fish such as sole (*sogliola*), red mullet (*triglia*), mullet (*céfalo*), sea bream (*orata*), monkfish (*coda di rospo*), and mackerel (*sgombro*). Fish is best eaten grilled (*alla griglia* or *ai ferri*). For a variety of fish and seafood opt for a *fritto di pesce* or *fritto misto di mare*, a plate of mixed fried fish and seafood. To round off a meal, sample Venice's well-known *tiramisù* (literally "pick me up"), usually a rum liqueur-laced pudding of sponge, mascarpone cheese, eggs, and chocolate.

BUDGET RESTAURANTS

Paying

The check (*il conto*) usually includes a cover charge per person (*pane e coperto*) and a 10–15 percent service charge (*servizio*). Restaurants are required by law to give you a proper receipt (*una ricevuta*). Always check the bill carefully, especially if—as still happens—it is an illegible scrawl on a piece of paper (strictly speaking illegal). Reduce costs by skipping *antipasti* and desserts—go to a *gelateria* for an ice-cream instead. Fixed-price tourist menus (*menù turistico*) usually include a basic pasta, main course, fruit, and half-bottles of wine and water. Food quality is often indifferent. The *prezzo fisso* menu usually excludes cover, service, and beverages. Check what is included in the price.

Remember that inexpensive snacks and meals are also available from cafés and wine bars (► 74–76).

ACIUGHETA
The "Little Anchovy" pizzeria-trattoria is one of the best places in the budget price range near Piazza San Marco.
➕ H12 ✉ Campo SS Filippo e Giacomo, Castello 4357 ☎ 522 4292 ⏰ Closed Wed in winter 🚤 San Zaccaria 1, 4, 52, 82

AI PROMESSI SPOSI
This friendly bar-restaurant serves up mainly fish dishes that are both inexpensive and come in huge portions. The snacks available from the bar are also excellent and even cheaper. An alternative to the nearby Casa Mia (see below).
➕ G10 ✉ Calle dell'Oca, Cannaregio 4367 ☎ 522 8609 ⏰ Closed Wed 🚤 Ca' d'Oro 1

AL GATTO NERO
This traditional trattoria has outside tables by the canal overlooking the old fish market opposite. This is the best place on Burano for simple, reasonably priced food.
➕ L2 ✉ Calle Stivallo-Fondamenta Giudecca, Burano 88 ☎ 730 120 ⏰ Closed Mon 🚤 Burano 12, 14

ALLA RIVETTA
A cheap but good-quality trattoria close to Piazza San Marco which makes a pleasant alternative to the nearby Aciugheta (see above). It is often busy.
➕ H12 ✉ Ponte San Provolo, near Campo SS Filippo e Giacomo, Castello 4625 ☎ 528 7302 ⏰ Closed Mon 🚤 San Zaccaria 1, 4, 52, 82

ALLE OCHE
Located just south of the quiet little square of Campo San Giacomo dell'Orio. Very popular, so reserve or arrive early to secure a table outside, and enjoy one of the many pizzas available.
➕ E10/11 ✉ Calle del Tintor, San Polo 1552 ☎ 524 1161 ⏰ Closed Mon 🚤 Riva di Biasio 1

ANTICO CAPON
A pleasant location on one of Venice's most attractive squares, plus pizzas cooked in a wood-fired oven (a rarity in fire-conscious Venice). In summer it has a few tables laid out on the piazza.
➕ D12 ✉ Campo Santa Margherita, Dorsoduro 3004/b ☎ 528 5292 ⏰ Closed Wed 🚤 San Tomà or Ca' Rezzonico 1, 82

CASA MIA
A popular and bustling pizzeria-trattoria with fine pizzas and good traditional Venetian dishes. Located in a little alley immediately west of the church of SS Apostoli.
➕ G10 ✉ Calle dell'Oca, Cannaregio 4430 ☎ 528 5590 ⏰ Closed Tue 🚤 Ca' d'Oro 1

CREPIZZA
This rather ordinary looking pizzeria-trattoria serves up wonderful pizzas and other simple fare. It is well placed for Santa Maria Gloriosa dei Frari and the Scuola

Grande di San Rocco, and is located just a few steps from the church of San Pantalon.

🔲 D/E12 ✉ Calle San Pantalon, Dorsoduro 3757 ☎ 524 2236 🕐 Closed Tue 🚤 San Tomà 1, 82

DONA ONESTA

The "Honest Woman" lives up to its name, offering good-quality food at budget prices. It is becoming increasingly well known, however, so try to reserve a table in its single small dining room. Overlooks a little canal midway between San Pantalon and San Tomà.

🔲 E12 ✉ Calle della Donna Onesta, Dorsoduro ☎ 522 9586 🕐 Closed Sun 🚤 San Tomà 1, 82

OSTERIA AI CACCIATORI

A pleasant old-fashioned establishment located on Murano's main canal in a street known for its glass shops. One of the few places to eat on the island.

🔲 K7/L6 ✉ Fondamenta dei Vetrai, Murano 69 🚤 Faro or Colonna 12, 13, 18, 52

ROSTICCERIA SAN BARTOLOMEO

A self-service place that is good for snacks, especially at lunchtime. There is no cover charge or service downstairs (the restaurant upstairs has almost the same food but at a higher price). Near the Rialto, off Campo San Bartolomeo.

🔲 G11 ✉ Calle della Bissa, San Marco 5424 ☎ 522 3569 🕐 Closed Mon 🚤 Rialto 1, 3, 82

TAVERNA SAN TROVASO

Not the best cuisine in the city, yet it offers reliable cooking at reasonable prices and is popular with local Venetians. Make a reservation to be sure of a place (especially for Sunday lunch) as its location west of the Accademia attracts passing trade.

🔲 E13 ✉ Fondamenta Priuli, Dorsoduro 1016 ☎ 520 3703 🕐 Closed Mon 🚤 Accademia 1, 3, 4, 82

TRATTORIA SAN TOMÀ

Although the pizzas and trattoria food served here are both good, this restaurant's best feature is its location on attractive Campo San Tomà, just one minute south of Santa Maria Gloriosa dei Frari and the Scuola Grande di San Rocco.

🔲 E12 ✉ Campo San Tomà, San Polo 2864 ☎ 710 586 🕐 Closed Tue in winter 🚤 San Tomà 1, 82

VIVALDI

This relaxed and pleasantly Venetian place produces simple hot dishes that can either be eaten standing at the front or sitting down at a few tables at the back, where more ambitious (and more expensive) meals are also on offer. Alternatively, you can just stop by for a glass of wine.

🔲 F11 ✉ Calle della Madonnetta, San Polo 1457 ☎ 523 8185 🚤 San Silvestro 1

Drinks

Venice's water is perfectly safe to drink, though Venetians prefer mineral water (*acqua minerale*) —either fizzy (*gassata*) or flat (*liscia, naturale*, or *non gassata*). Bottles come in one liter (*un litro* or *una bottiglia*) or half-liter (*mezzo litro* or *mezza bottiglia*) sizes. Bottled fruit juice is *un succo di frutta*, available in pear (*pera*), apricot (*albiccoca*), peach (*pesca*), and other flavors. Fresh juice is *una spremuta*, while milk shake is *un frullato*, or *un frappé* if made with ice cream. *Lemon Soda* is a popular and refreshing bitter-lemon drink. Ice is *ghiaccio*, and a slice of lemon is *uno spicchio di limone*.

CAFÉS, BARS, & GELATERIE

Etiquette

The procedure when standing up in a bar is to pay for what you want at the cash desk (*la cassa*) and take your receipt (*lo scontrino*) to the bar, where you repeat your order (a L200 tip slapped down on the bar works wonders with the service). Do *not* then take your drink and sit at outside tables, as you almost always pay a premium to sit down, when you order through a waiter. Sitting, a single purchase allows you to watch the world go by almost indefinitely. Ice cream (*un gelato*) comes in a cone (*un cono*) or a tub (*una coppa*): specify which you want, along with a price (quantity and tub size rise in L500 intervals from about L2,000 to 4,000). You are also often asked if you want cream (*panna*) on top, which is usually free.

CA' D'ORO

This wonderfully fusty and very Venetian place has been owned by the same family for 120 years. Also known as La Vedova ("The Widow"), it produces snacks and basic hot meals.
⊞ G10 ⊠ Calle del Pistor-Ramo Ca' d'Oro, Cannaregio ⊘ Closed Sun and Thu ⊟ Ca' d'Oro 1

CAFFÈ DEI FRARI

If you do not want to walk to Ciak (see below), try this lively bar just across the bridge in front of the façade of Santa Maria Gloriosa dei Frari. It is a favorite with students from the university.
⊞ E11 ⊠ Fondamenta dei Frari, San Polo 2564 ⊟ San Tomà 1, 82

CAUSIN

Opened in 1928, this is one of several excellent cafés on Venice's nicest square. Great ice cream and plenty of outdoor tables.
⊞ D12 ⊠ Campo Santa Margherita, Dorsoduro 2996 ⊟ Ca' Rezzonico 1

CIAK

A pleasant and relaxed bar to retire to after seeing Santa Maria Gloriosa dei Frari and the Scuola Grande di San Rocco. Used by everyone from gondoliers to society ladies. Good lunchtime snacks and sandwiches.
⊞ E12 ⊠ Campo San Tomà, San Polo 280 ⊟ San Tomà 1, 82

FLORIAN

The oldest, prettiest, and most expensive of Venice's famous big-league cafés has been serving customers since 1720. Very high prices, but worth treating yourself at least once for the experience and the chance to admire the lovely frescoed and mirrored interior.
⊞ G12 ⊠ Piazza San Marco, San Marco 56–59 ⊘ Closed Wed ⊟ San Marco 1, 3, 4, 82

HARRY'S BAR

One of Venice's (and Europe's) most famous bars, known for its top-notch cocktails as well as its highly rated food (▶ 69). Be certain to dress up and be prepared for high prices and lots of foreigners.
⊞ G12/13 ⊠ Calle Vallaresso, San Marco 1323 ⊟ San Marco 1, 3, 4, 82

HARRY'S DOLCI

This offshoot of Harry's Bar began as a fancy coffee shop, but now serves meals as well (▶ 69). It remains a good place to treat yourself to a morning coffee or afternoon tea in refined but unintimidating surroundings.
⊞ D14 ⊠ Fondamenta San Biagio, Giudecca 773 ☎ 522 4844 ⊘ Apr–Oct: daily 10:30AM–3PM, 7:30–10:30PM. Nov–Mar: closed Tue ⊟ Sant'Eufemia 52, 82

IL CAFFÈ

Another appealing and photogenic little bar on Campo Santa Margherita. Its outside tables are a favorite place to soak up the sun and streetlife.
⊞ D12 ⊠ Campo Santa

WIN

Margherita, Dorsoduro 2963
Ca' Rezzonico 1

MARCHINI

This café-*pasticceria* just east of Campo Santo Stefano (Campo Francesco Morosini) is widely regarded as Venice's best. The mouth-watering window displays alone are worth a special visit. Eat in with a coffee or drink, or order a takeout.
F12/13 Ponte San Maurizio, San Marco 2769
Santa Maria del Giglio 1

NICO

Organize a walk or stroll in the San Polo or Dorsoduro districts so that you pass this small waterfront bar, which is renowned for its ice cream, in particular a praline concoction known as *gianduiotto*.
E14 Zattere ai Gesuati, Dorsoduro 922 Closed Thu
Zattere 52, 82

PAOLIN

The best café in one of Venice's nicest squares. Lots of outside tables, and some of the city's best ice cream to eat in or takeout.
F12 Campo Santo Stefano (Campo Francesco Morosini), San Marco 2962
Closed Fri Accademia 1, 3, 4, 82

PARADISO PERDUTO

A good choice of bar both day and night if you want to rub shoulders with the more arty and Bohemian of Venice's inhabitants. Lively late-night atmosphere, and you'll find meals and snacks at shared wooden tables and

the occasional live music, usually on Sundays.
F9 Fondamenta della Misericordia, Cannaregio 2540
Closed Wed San Marcuola 1, 82

QUADRI

Not as long-established or attractive as Florian, and not quite as famous or socially exalted. It was abandoned by Venetian high society in the 19th century because it was frequented by officers of the occupying Austrian army. Prices, however, reach the Florian's stratospheric levels.
G12 Piazza San Marco, San Marco 120–4 San Marco 1, 3, 4, 82

ROSA SALVA

Venice's best café chain has outlets throughout the city. Coffees and cakes are good, but the atmosphere can sometimes be a bit lacking.
G12 Campo San Luca, San Marco Rialto 1, 3, 82.
G11/12 Merceria San Salvador, San Marco 951
Rialto 1, 3, 82. G12
Calle Fiubera, San Marco
San Marco 1, 3, 4, 82

VINO VINO

Rather more showy and pretentious than some of Venice's humbler bars, but offers a choice of over 100 different wines to accompany its middling snacks and meals. Located close to La Fenice opera house.
F12 Ponte delle Veste, Calle delle Veste, San Marco 2007
Closed Tue Santa Maria del Giglio

Coffee

At breakfast you will be served a milky *cappuccino*, named after the brown robes and white cowls of Capuchin monks. During the rest of the day the locals' coffee of choice is the short, black *espresso* or *un caffè*. A longer *espresso* is a *lungo* or a *doppia* (double). Decaffeinated coffee is *un caffè Hag*, iced coffee *caffè freddo*, and American-style coffee (not as strong as the Italian brews) is *un caffè Americano*. Other varieties on offer include *caffè corretto* (with a dash of grappa or brandy), *caffè latte* (a longer *cappuccino*), and *caffè macchiato* (an espresso "stained" with a drop of milk). Note that Italians rarely drink *cappuccino* after midday—and never after a meal, when they opt for *espresso* or camomile tea (*una camomila*) instead.

BARS

Wine bars

Old-fashioned wine bars, or *bacari*, are a Venetian way of life. One of the city's more civilized habits is the custom of breaking up the day with an *ombra* ("shadow"), a small glass of wine that takes its name from the idea of escaping the heat of the sun for a restorative tipple. A small snack, or *cichetto*, usually accompanies the drink. An *enoteca* is a more refined bar, with a greater choice of wines and a range of reasonably priced snacks and hot meals.

AL VOLTO

A genuine *enoteca* (see panel) located north of Campo Manin. Good snacks and a staggering 1,300 different wines from Italy and the rest of the world.
➕ F12 ✉ Calle Cavalli, San Marco 4081 🕐 Closed Sun 🚢 Rialto 1, 3, 82

ANTICA DOLO

The Rialto market district has one of the city's largest selections of old-fashioned wine bars. This, along with the nearby Do Mori (see below), is one of the best.
➕ F11 ✉ Ruga Vecchia San Giovanni, San Polo 778 🕐 Closed Sun 🚢 Rialto 1, 3, 82

BOLDRIN

Excellent and roomy *enoteca* in the northern part of the city. Wine is served by the glass and you can order hot snacks.
➕ G11 ✉ Salizzada San Chianciano, Cannaregio 5550 🕐 Closed Sun 🚢 Rialto 1, 3, 82

CANTINA DEL VINO GIÀ SCHIAVI

An old-fashioned wine shop that really looks the part, set almost opposite San Trovaso and one of Venice's few remaining gondola workshops.
➕ E13 ✉ Fondamenta Nani-Meravegie, Dorsoduro 992 🕐 Closed Sun 🚢 Accademia 1, 3, 4, 82

DO MORI

The most authentic and atmospheric of Venice's old-time *bacari*, in business since 1462. Always filled with locals, shoppers, and traders from the nearby Rialto markets. Good snacks, 350 wines, but no seats or tables.
➕ F11 ✉ Calle do Mori, off Ruga Vecchia San Giovanni, San Polo 429 🕐 Daily 9–1, 5–8. Closed Sun, Wed afternoon 🚢 Rialto 1, 3, 82

DO SPADE

Do Spade is not quite as hectic and nicely down-at-heel as the nearby Do Mori (see above), but is almost as busy and equally authentic and old-fashioned. Unlike its neighbor it also has tables. Difficult to find.
➕ F11 ✉ Sottoponego Spade, off Calle Angelo, San Polo 860 🕐 Sep–Jun: Mon–Wed, Fri–Sat 9–2, 5–11; Thu 9–2. Jul–Aug: Mon–Wed, Fri–Sat 9–2, 5–8; Thu 9–2. Closed Sun 🚢 Rialto 1, 3, 82

OSTERIA AGLI ASSASSINI

This wine bar is located between Campo Manin and Campo Sant'Angelo, and has a good selection of wines, light snacks, and basic meals.
➕ F12 ✉ Rio Terrà degli Assassini, San Marco 3695 🕐 Closed Sun 🚢 Sant'Angelo 1

OSTERIA ALLE BOTTEGHE

A lively and very busy place just north of Campo Santo Stefano (Campo Francesco Morosini). Plenty of wines to choose from and a small selection of snacks.
➕ F12 ✉ Calle delle Botteghe, San Marco 🕐 Closed Sun 🚢 Sant'Angelo or San Samuele 1, 3, 4, 82

GLASS & BEADS

ANTICLEA ANTIQUARIATO

This beautiful little shop is an absolute treasure trove of antique Venetian beads and jewelry. The owner has spent a lifetime amassing her stock, the best of which is kept in countless small drawers around the walls. Beads of your choice can be made up on the spot into earrings or necklaces.

⊞ H12 ⊠ Campo San Provolo, Castello 4719a ☎ 528 6946 ⊟ San Zaccaria 1, 4, 52, 82

BAROVIER E TOSO

One of the better of the many glass showrooms on the island of Murano, this family firm dates back to the 14th century and makes glass to traditional designs, drawing its inspiration from a private 26,000-piece collection of antique glass.

⊞ K7/L6 ⊠ Fondamenta dei Vetrai, Murano 28 ☎ 739 049 ⊟ Colonna or Faro 12, 52

L'ISOLA

Grotesque modern glass litters countless Venetian shops and souvenir stands. This shop has some of the city's better contemporary designs, although you may still find some of them too far-fetched. As is the case with much Venetian glass, prices can be surprisingly high.

⊞ G12 ⊠ Salizzada San Moisè, San Marco 1468 ⊟ San Marco 1, 3, 4, 82

PAOLO ROSSI

This appealing shop (located just east of Piazza San Marco) specializes in convincing reproductions of antique glass and designs. As a result its product is less gaudy than some shops.

⊞ H12 ⊠ Campo di San Zaccaria, San Marco 4685 ☎ 522 7005 ⊟ San Zaccaria 1, 4, 52, 82

SALVIATI

Founded in 1866, Salviati is known for having provided the eye-catching mosaics on the façade of the Grand Canal's Palazzo Salviati, located on the south bank close to the Palazzo Dario. It has outlets in Murano and in Venice proper.

⊞ F13 ⊠ Campo Santa Maria Zobenigo, San Marco 2461 ☎ 522 6332 ⊟ Santa Maria del Giglio 1

SEGUSO

Another of Murano's better and longer-established institutions, Seguso has been in business for several decades. It is particularly renowned for its copies of antique glass.

⊞ L6 ⊠ Ponte Longo (Ponte Vivarini), Murano 138 ☎ 739 423 ⊟ Colonna or Faro 12, 52

VENINI

A Murano institution since the 1930s attracting some of the top names in glass design. More upscale and daring designs than many producers.

⊞ G12 ⊠ Piazzetta dei Leoni (Piazzetta dei Leoncini), San Marco 314 ☎ 522 4045 ⊟ San Marco 1, 3, 4, 82
⊞ K7/L6 ⊠ Fondamenta dei Vetrai, Murano 50 ⊟ Colonna, Faro or Museo 12, 52

Poison daggers

Murano glass was said to be so fine that it would shatter on coming into contact with even the smallest drop of poison. It was also used in the Venetian dagger, one of the Middle Ages' nastier weapons. Much loved by Venice's secret police, the dagger consisted of a razor-sharp blade of glass, sheathed in metal, which when sunk into a victim's body would snap off at the haft. The unfortunate's skin would close over the glass, leaving a wound apparently no more than an innocent graze at the point of entry.

Window-Shopping

Department stores

Venice is hard done by when it comes to both supermarkets and department stores. The only large department store worthy of the name is the excellent COIN, which sells a wide range of fashion, toiletries, accessories, china, linen, gifts, and general goods. It occupies a large corner block on the east side of Salizzada San Giovanni Crisostomo between the Rialto and the church of San Giovanni Crisostomo (✚ G11).

Where to look

Fine stores can be found across Venice, but the city's better stores (especially for shoes and fashion) cluster in well-defined areas such as the Calle dei Fabbri (✚ G12); Calle dell'Ascensione-Calle Larga (Viale) XXII Marzo (✚ F13/G12); the Frezzeria (✚ G12); and the so-called Mercerie—San Zulian, d'Orologio and San Salvador—which run from Piazza San Marco to the Rialto (✚ G12).

EMILIO CECCATO
If there is one Venetian souvenir, over and above glass, that greets you at every turn in Venice, it is the fake and mass-produced gondolier's straw hat. If you abhor fakes, head for this unique little shop, which sells genuine gondoliers' garb—hats, tunics, and trousers—to both gondoliers and curious foreigners.
✚ G11 ✉ Sottoportico di Rialto, San Polo 1617 ☎ 522 2700 🚤 Rialto 1, 3, 82

EMPORIO ARMANI
No leading Italian city would be complete without a flagship store dedicated to one of the most famous names in Italian fashion. In Venice, Armani's store is in one of the city's main shopping streets, located a short walk from Piazza San Marco. The clothes here are peerless, classic, and exquisitely cut.
✚ G12 ✉ Calle dei Fabbri, San Marco 989 ☎ 523 7808 🚤 Rialto 1, 3, 82

FIORELLA
Hilarious and wonderfully original, Fiorella on the east side of the square wins the title of Venice's best-dressed window hands down: the shop dummies, crafted in wood, represent life-sized models of former doges, each incongruously decked out in high heels and other slightly offbeat high fashion items.
✚ F12 ✉ Campo Santo Stefano (Campo Francesco Morosini), San Marco 2806 ☎ 520 9228 🚤 Accademia 1, 3, 4, 82

JESURUM
Factory-made (and often foreign-manufactured) lace has undercut and largely supplanted the famous traditional hand-made lace of Burano (▶ 20). As a result, original and old-style lace is now extremely rare and expensive. However, this store, close to the Rialto bridge, has an excellent selection of both types of lace, plus a fine collection of superb linens and lingerie. Other little shops selling lace, often at keen prices, can be found dotted around the city. Place-settings and similar small pieces make excellent gifts.
✚ G11 ✉ Merceria del Capitello, San Marco 4857 ☎ 520 6177 🚤 Rialto 1, 3, 82

LA PANTOFOLA
Come here for fine shoes and even better traditional Venetian velvet slippers —which make excellent and unusual gifts—in a wide range of bright colors.
✚ F12 ✉ Calle della Mandola, San Marco 3718 ☎ 522 2150 🚤 Sant'Angelo 1

LABORATORIO ARTIGIANO MASCHERE
This wonderful mask workshop, located just east of SS Giovanni e Paolo, is home to Giorgio Clanetti, scion of a family of puppet makers, who was one of the first to resurrect the Venetian tradition of maskmaking.
✚ H/J11 ✉ Barbaria delle Tole, Castello 3063 ☎ 522 3110 🚤 Ospedale 23, 52

LAURA BIAGIOTTA

One of the big names in Italian high fashion, Biagiotti is located in the heart of one of the city's most exclusive shopping streets, a thoroughfare which runs west from Piazza San Marco.

⊞ F13/G12 ✉ Calle Larga (Viale) XXII Marzo, San Marco 2400/a ☎ 520 3401 🚤 San Marco 1, 3, 4, 82

MISSIAGLIA

Missiaglia's superlative gold and silver jewelry means it is widely considered the city's finest jeweler. However, its Piazza San Marco setting means that bargains are few and far between.

⊞ G12 ✉ Procuratie Vecchie, Piazza San Marco 125 ☎ 522 4464 🚤 San Marco 1, 3, 4, 82

MISSONI

Another of the big Italian fashion names, best known for highly colored knitwear and similarly innovative linens, bedwear, and casualwear.

⊞ G12/13 ✉ Calle Vallaresso, San Marco 1312 ☎ 520 5733 🚤 San Marco 1, 3, 4, 82

MONDO NOVO

The masks in this attractive shop just south of Campo Santa Margherita are definitely superior to the more run-of-the-mill versions found in lesser shops dotted around the city. The store is a wonderful place for children and adults alike to browse.

⊞ D12 ✉ Rio Terrà Canal, Dorsoduro 3063 ☎ 287 344 🚤 Ca' Rezzonico 1

NARDI

Rivals Missiaglia (see above) for the title of Venice's smartest jewelers. Its Piazza San Marco location obviously ensures the highest prices.

⊞ G12 ✉ Procuratie Nuove, Piazza San Marco ☎ 522 5733 🚤 San Marco 1, 3, 4, 82

RUBELLI

Rubelli has been turning out stunning traditional fabrics since 1850. However, as many of its skilled workers are retiring there is talk of transforming the workshop into a museum.

⊞ F12 ✉ Palazzo Corner Spinelli, Calle dell'Albero, Sant'Angelo, San Marco 3877 ☎ 521 6411 🚤 Sant'Angelo 1

TROIS

Venice's former trade in silks, damasks, and other exotic materials is still reflected in shops selling a host of fine fabrics. The best known is perhaps Trois, whose specialization in old fabrics includes exclusive rights to some of Fortuny's famous silks (see panel).

⊞ F13 ✉ Campo San Maurizio 2666 ☎ 522 2905 🚤 Santa Maria del Giglio 1

VALENTINO

The doyen of Rome *alta moda* and high-quality ready-to-wear clothes has a shop just west of Piazza San Marco close to other leading names in the world of high fashion.

⊞ G12 ✉ Salizzada San Moisè, San Marco 1473 ☎ 520 5733 🚤 San Marco 1, 3, 4, 82

Mariano Fortuny

Fortuny was born in Catalonia in 1871, the son of a painter and fabric collector. He moved to Venice when he was 18, soon gaining renown in fields ranging from physics and chemistry to architecture and theater design. Today, he is best remembered for his fabrics, and in particular for the pleated dresses he created that were so fine they could be rolled up and threaded through a wedding ring. Sadly, none of his famous dresses features among the interesting and unusual items on display in the Museo Fortuny

⊞ F12 ✉ Palazzo Pesaro, Campo San Benedetto, San Marco 3780 🕐 Tue–Sun 9–7 🚤 Sant'Angelo 1 💰 Expensive.

BOOKS, PAPER, & STATIONERY

Antiques

Bric-à-brac and antique bargains are rare in a city that is acutely aware of its past and the value of its *objets d'art*. If you have money to spare, however, Venice offers an almost unlimited choice of beautiful things to buy. Antique shops are dotted around the city, but the largest concentrations are found around San Maurizio and Santa Maria Zobenigo just east of Campo Santo Stefano (Campo Francesco Morosini; ➕ F12/13). Slightly less expensive shops can be found in the area around San Barnaba (➕ D12). The most famous shops are Paolo Scarpa's two outlets at Campo San Moisè, San Marco 1464 (➕ G12), and Calle Larga (Viale) XXII Marzo, San Marco 2089 (➕ F13/G12). Regular flea and antique markets are held in Campo San Maurizio; contact the tourist office for details of forthcoming dates.

ALBERTO VALESE

Valese was at the cutting edge of the revival in traditional Venetian marbled paper that took place in the 1970s. He has two outlets for his marbled paper, fabrics, and ornaments (see also Ebrû below).

➕ F12 ✉ Campiello Santo Stefano, San Marco 3471 ☎ 520 0921 🚤 Sant'Angelo or Accademia 1, 3, 4, 82

EBRÛ

Alberto Valese's second shop takes its name from the traditional Turkish marbling technique used to create many of his products. Some of the smaller items make ideal gifts or souvenirs to take home.

➕ F13 ✉ Calle del Teatro, San Marco 2052 ☎ 528 6302 🚤 Santa Maria del Giglio 1

FANTONI

If you want to take home pictures of some of the paintings you have seen in Venice, this well-known shop contains the city's largest selection of big, glossy art books.

➕ F/G12 ✉ Salizzada San Luca, San Marco 4119 ☎ 522 0700 🚤 Rialto 1, 3, 82

FILIPPI EDITORE VENEZIA

This specialist shop is renowned for its large collection of books on all aspects of Venice (mostly in Italian) and its many facsimile editions of old books.

➕ G11 ✉ Calle della Casselleria, San Marco 5284 ☎ 523 6916 🚤 Rialto 1, 3, 82

GOLDONI

Well stocked and by common consent the best general bookstore in the city, Goldini has a wide range of literature on the city, along with a limited selection of foreign-language titles (including English).

➕ G12 ✉ Calle dei Fabbri, San Marco 4742 ☎ 522 2384 🚤 San Marco 1, 3, 4, 82

LEGATORIA PIAZZESI

This is one of the last workshops in the city to use traditional wood-block methods for hand-printing papers, books, and stationery. Its beautiful products are expensive.

➕ F12 ✉ Campiello della Feltrina, San Marco 2511 ☎ 522 1202 🚤 Santa Maria del Giglio 1

PAOLO OLBI

Like Valese (see above), Olbi was at the forefront of the revival in traditional marbled papers. His appealing shop sells a wide range of marbled stationery and ornaments.

➕ F12 ✉ Calle della Mandola, San Marco 3653 ☎ 528 5025 🚤 Sant'Angelo 1

POLLIERO

A tiny, old-fashioned shop right alongside Santa Maria Gloriosa dei Frari, Polliero sells a lovely selection of leather-bound and marbled paper stationery, together with hand-made gifts and beautiful individual sheets of paper.

➕ E11 ✉ Campo dei Frari, San Polo 2995 ☎ 528 5130 🚤 San Tomà 1, 82

FOOD & DRINK

ALIANI (CASA DEL PARMIGIANO)

Perhaps Venice's most famous delicatessen, this shop has a superlative selection of cheeses, together with a variety of hams, salamis, fresh pasta, and other ready-made delicacies.

➕ F11 ✉ Campo della Corderia, Ruga Vecchia San Giovanni, San Polo 214 ☎ 520 6525 🚤 Rialto or San Silvestro 1, 3, 82

ERBERIA

Venice's main outdoor market provides a wonderful spectacle of sound and color, its stalls laden with fruit and vegetables, its thoroughfares busy with shoppers and traders. Be sure to explore the maze of stalls north of Campo San Giacomo di Rialto, not merely the more touristy stalls that line the Ruga degli Orefici.

➕ G11 ✉ Campo San Giacomo di Rialto 🕐 Mon–Sat 7–1 🚤 Rialto 1, 3, 82

MARKETS

Market stalls can be found in the following locations: Campo Santa Margherita (➕ D12); Campo Santa Maria Formosa (➕ H11); Campiello dell'Anconetta-Rio Terrà San Leonardo (➕ E9); the boats moored on Rio della Tana (➕ K/L13); and, most evocatively, the famous covered barge by the Ponte dei Pugni on Fondamenta Gerardini (➕ D12).

MASCARI

A speciality food shop near the Rialto known for its range of teas, coffees, seeds, and dried goods.

➕ F11 ✉ Ruga dei Spezieri, San Polo 380 ☎ 522 9762 🚤 Rialto or San Silvestro 1, 3, 82

PASTICCERIA MARCHINI

Delicious cakes, cookies, pastries, and sweetmeats from Venice's finest *pasticceria*.

➕ F13 ✉ Ponte San Maurizio, San Marco 2769 ☎ 522 9109 🚤 Santa Maria del Giglio 1

PESCHERIA

Venice's evocative fish market, its stalls loaded with all manner of exotic-looking fish and seafood, merges seamlessly with the fruit and vegetable stalls of the adjoining Erberia (see above).

➕ F/G11 ✉ Campo della Pescaria 🕐 Tue–Sat 7–1 🚤 Rialto 1, 3, 82

WINE

Old-fashioned wine shops, where you can take empty bottles to be filled from wooden barrels or wicker-wrapped vats, still dot most Venetian neighborhoods. The wine—which can also be bought in bottles—is inexpensive and of good quality, and embraces most of the Veneto's many varieties, including some that are hard to find elsewhere. Wine bars also sell wine by the bottle to take away (▶ 76). The following La Nave d'Oro outlets are typical.

➕ D12 ✉ Campo Santa Margherita, Dorsoduro 3664. ➕ H11 ✉ Calle del Mondo Novo, Castello 5786. ➕ E9 ✉ Rio Terrà San Leonardo, Cannaregio 1370

Practicalities

Food shops and bakeries are usually open 8:30–1 and 4–7, though virtually all close on Wednesday afternoons and Sundays. Food served by weight (including bread) is sold by the *chilo*, *mezzo chilo* (kilo and half-kilo: about 2lb. and 1lb.) and, more commonly, by the *etto* (100g: about 4oz.), plural *etti*.

The Rialto

As a district the Rialto is almost as old as the city itself, the earliest settlers having been attracted to its high banks, or *rivo alto*, these forming a dry and easily defended redoubt amidst the marsh and mud of the lagoon. While San Marco developed into the city's political heart, the Rivoaltus became its commercial center, where all manner of staple and exotic goods were traded in the "Bazaar of Europe." The first private banks appeared here in 1157, these soon followed (in 1161) by the Banco di Piazza, Europe's state bank. It did not take long for the tax collectors, magistrates and other offices of state to appear in their wake.

AFTER DARK

What's on

Details of films, concerts, and exhibitions in Venice can be found in the *"Spettacoli"* section of daily editions of local newspapers such as *Il Gazzettino* and *La Nuova Venezia. Un Ospite di Venezia*, a free Italian/English magazine available from hotels and tourist offices, also contains detailed listings (published weekly in high season, monthly in low season). Tourist offices always have plenty of posters and leaflets on current events. Also keep an eye open for posters on the streets.

CASINÒ

Venice's popular Casinò Municipale (Municipal Casino), one of only a handful in Italy, is housed in winter in the Palazzo Vendramin-Calergi, one of the Grand Canal's most impressive palaces. From mid-June until mid-September it moves to the Lido at the Palazzo del Casinò. Dress is smart, and you should take along your passport.

✚ F9/10 ✉ Palazzo Vendramin-Calergi, Calle Larga Vendramin, off Rio Terrà della Maddalena, Cannaregio ☎ 710 211 ⏱ Mid-Sep–mid-Jun, daily 4PM–2:30AM ⛴ San Marcuola 1, 82 ❓ Dress code. ✚ J/K17 ✉ Palazzo del Casinò, Piazzale del Casinò, Lungomare G Marconi, Lido ☎ 529 7111 ⏱ Mid-Jun–mid-Sep, daily 4PM–2:30AM ⛴ Casinò or Santa Maria Elisabetta 1, 6, 40, 41, 52, 82 ❓ Dress code

CINEMA

Considering the fact that Venice hosts one of Europe's leading film festivals, it seems astonishing that it has just five movie theaters. Art-house, classic, or original-language films are screened occasionally at the so-called Cinema d'Essai, but virtually all foreign and current-release films are dubbed into Italian. The city's principal cinemas are listed below.

Accademia: ✚ E13 ✉ Calle Corfù, Dorsoduro 1019 ☎ 528 7706 ⛴ Accademia 1, 3, 4, 82
Centrale: ✚ G12 ✉ Piscina da Frezzeria, San Marco 1659 ☎ 522 8201 ⛴ San Marco 1, 3, 4, 82

Olimpia: ✚ G12 ✉ Campo San Gallo o Canova, San Marco 1094 ☎ 520 5439 ⛴ San Marco 1, 3, 4, 82
Ritz: ✚ G12 ✉ Calle dei Segretaria, near Campo San Zulian, San Marco 617 ☎ 520 4429 ⛴ San Marco 1, 3, 4, 82
Rossini: ✚ E12 ✉ Calle delle Muneghe, San Marco 4000 ☎ 523 0322 ⛴ San Samuele 3, 4, 82

CLASSICAL MUSIC

Venice's main classical music spot is La Fenice (see "Opera" below), a lovely building which, until it was gutted by fire, presented a winter opera season and a summer season of miscellaneous classical concerts. In its (temporary) absence the city's main classical music venue is La Pietà, Vivaldi's former church, which presents regular concerts of the Venetian composer's work plus other occasional recitals. Tickets are rather expensive, and often pricier than the performance merits. Concerts are also held in the churches of San Stae, Santo Stefano, and Santa Maria Gloriosa dei Frari, San Barnaba and the Ospedaletto, and at the Palazzo Prigione Vecchie, the Palasport dell'Arsenale, and the Scuola Grande di San Giovanni Evangelista. Keep your eyes open for posters advertising concerts, or inquire at the tourist office regarding forthcoming events (▶ 87).

The state radio network, RAI, allows the public into recordings of its concerts in the Palazzo

Labia, though the free tickets must be reserved in advance (see below). Several small foundations also organize occasional recitals, most notably the Cini Foundation, based at San Giorgio Maggiore, and the Ugo and Olga Levi Foundation, based at the Palazzo Giustinian-Lolin (enquire at the tourist office for details). The Amici della Musica is a "club" next to the Miracoli church which holds small concerts, art exhibitions, and nightly readings of prose and poetry.

Amici della Musica: 🕀 G11 ✉ Campo Miracoli ☎ 528 7986 🚤 Rialto 1, 3, 82

La Pietà (Santa Maria della Pietà o della Visitazione): 🕀 H12 ✉ Riva degli Schiavoni ☎ 520 4431 🚤 San Zaccaria 1, 4, 52, 82 ❓ Tickets expensive

RAI: 🕀 E9 ✉ Palazzo Labia, Campo San Geremia ☎ 716 666 🚤 Ferrovia 1, 3, 4, 52, 82

CLUBS

Venice has a reputation as a rather sleepy place, and young Venetians often complain about its lack of nightlife. The majority of the region's big discos and clubs are in Mestre and distant Jesolo on the mainland (see newspaper listings for details), while the closest any big bands get to the city for concerts is Padua or Verona. Venice's only "disco" is the rather unhip Il Piccolo Mondo (see below). Livelier and more fashionable are Round Midnight, a bar-club with dancing, and the atmospheric Paradiso

Perduto, a bar-restaurant with occasional live music (see below). Harry's Dolci, on the Giudecca, is a smart café-restaurant that has occasional jazz concerts to accompany its cakes, pastries, and meals.

Harry's Dolci: 🕀 D14 ✉ Fondamenta San Biagio, Giudecca 773 ☎ 522 4844 🕐 Apr–Oct: daily 10:30AM–3PM, 7:30–10:30PM. Nov–Mar: closed Tue 🚤 Sant'Eufemia 52, 82

Il Piccolo Mondo: 🕀 E13 ✉ Calle Corfù, Dorsoduro 1056/a ☎ 520 0371 🕐 Bar: 10AM–8PM. Disco: 10PM–4AM 🚤 Accademia 1, 3, 4, 82

Paradiso Perduto: 🕀 F9 ✉ Fondamenta della Misericordia, Cannaregio 2540 ☎ 720 581 🕐 Closed Wed 🚤 San Marcuola or Madonna dell' Orto 1, 52, 82

Round Midnight: 🕀 E13 ✉ Fondamenta dello Squero, Dorsoduro 3102 ☎ 523 1078 🕐 Nightly except Wed 🚤 Ca' Rezzonico 1

OPERA

The catastrophic fire at La Fenice ("The Phoenix") on January 29, 1996 has put Venice's famous opera house out of action for the foreseeable future. Plans to rebuild and restore its once magnificent interior are well advanced, though it is almost impossible to know when the hall will finally reopen for performances. In the meantime, temporary venues have been arranged for opera performances.

🕀 F12 ✉ Teatro La Fenice, Campo San Fantin, San Marco 1965 ☎ 521 0161; fax 522 1768 🚤 Santa Maria del Giglio 1

Evening pastimes

Venice does not have the nightlife to match other major cities. For many Venetians an evening out consists of a meal or drink with friends rounded off with a stroll to a bar for a coffee or ice cream. One of the best places to join them is Campo Santa Margherita, a square full of easy-going bars and cafés in the student district of Dorsoduro (🕀 D12). Other similar squares include Campo San Polo (🕀 E/F11), Campo Santo Stefano (Campo Francesco Morosini; 🕀 F12), Campo San Barnaba (🕀 D12) and Campo Santa Maria Formosa (🕀 H11). If all you want to do is walk, few cities can compare with Venice when it comes to atmospheric evening strolls, and none can offer the experience of a gondola or *vaporetto* ride on the Grand Canal.

FESTIVALS

Regata Storica

The Regata Storica ("Historic Regatta"; first Sunday in September) is the most famous of several annual regattas held in and around the city each year. A huge flotilla of beautifully decorated craft, their crews in period dress, travels in colorful procession down the Grand Canal (note that onlookers are expected to dress the part too). Races are then held, the most exciting being those between rival gondoliers.

Marriage to the Sea

This ceremony began in AD 997, when Doge Pietro Orseolo II set sail to attack Dalmatia, among the first of Venice's conquests. Originally a libation before battle, in time it came to symbolize the Republic's naval power and special relationship with the sea. The doge and his retinue would sail into the lagoon, there dropping a golden ring into the water and reciting the words: "We espouse thee, O sea, in sign of our real and perpetual dominion over thee." Divers then competed to find the ring, the winner—if any—earning relief from "all the burdens to which dwellers in the Republic are subject."

CARNIVAL

Venice's famous carnival takes its name from the Latin *carnem levare*, or *carne vale*—the "farewell to meat." It probably began in the city's 15th-century private clubs, whose members indicated their allegiances by wearing different colored hose. Although the clubs initially limited themselves to boat races and social frivolities, they eventually took to competing in masked balls on Martedì Grasso, the prelude to Lent. Resurrected as recently as 1979 (by a group of non-Venetians), it emulates the great pre-Lenten festivals of the 18th century, thousands of tourists dressing in masks and extravagant costumes to indulge in a series of enthusiastically supported events. Today, the carnival officially lasts just ten days (up to the beginning of Lent), though the event has become so large —and so commercialized—that Venice often has to close the causeway to cars for the duration.

FESTA DEL REDENTORE

The Festa del Redentore is the more spectacular of the two major festivals held to celebrate Venice's deliverance from past epidemics (the other is the Festa della Salute; see below). Observed on the third Sunday of July, it commemorates the end of the 1576 plague, an epidemic that wiped out a third of the city's inhabitants. In times past the doge and his entourage would visit the church of the Redentore, crossing to the Giudecca on a pontoon of boats thrown across the Canale della Giudecca. Today, Venetians stream across a similar bridge on the Saturday evening, many taking to boats for a traditional picnic on the water.

FESTA DELLA SALUTE

Like the Festa del Redentore, the feast of La Salute (November 21) commemorates Venice's deliverance from bubonic plague, in this case the epidemic of 1630 which claimed an estimated one-third of the city's population. Ever since, Venetians have crossed a pontoon bridge thrown across the Grand Canal to Santa Maria della Salute (built to mark the end of the plague; ➤ 34), to offer thanks for their health (*salute*) and to pray for sick friends and relations.

LA SENSA

The feast of the La Sensa (Sunday after Ascension Day) is a resurrected version of the ancient Marriage to the Sea ceremony (see panel). The city mayor, his or her retinue and assorted VIPs sail out onto the lagoon on a copy of the *Bucintoro*, the old dogal state barge. Also in May is the more impressive Vogalonga, or "Long Row," during which boats compete in a 20 mile race to the island of Burano and back.

VENICE
travel facts

DOGE CALIMERO

ARRIVING & DEPARTING

Before you go

- US, EU, and Commonwealth citizens require a passport for visits to Italy.
- Visas are usually required for nationals of other countries.

When to go

- Try to avoid July and August, the hottest and busiest months, and plan a visit for April, May, June, September or October.
- Hotels are busy from Easter to October, in February during Carnevale, and over Christmas and New Year.
- Despite the weather, winter can still be a delightful time to see the city.

Climate

- Venice has generally mild winters and warm summers, but the latter can be hot and oppressive, with occasional thunderstorms (especially in September), while winter temperatures often match those of northern European cities. A chill easterly wind, the *bora*, can lower temperatures in spring and autumn.
- Outside the summer months, fog is a common phenomenon.
- Flooding (*acqua alta*) can occur any time, but especially between November and March.

Arriving by air

- Scheduled internal and international flights (plus a few charters) arrive at Venice's Marco Polo Airport, 5 miles north of the city centre (☎ 260 9260 or 260 6111).
- Most charters arrive at Treviso, 19 miles from Venice. A shuttlebus runs to Treviso town center, from where there are regular bus and train connections to Venice.
- Connections from Marco Polo to

Venice's Piazzale Roma (20 minutes) can be made by taxi, by blue ATVO buses, or by the less expensive and less-frequent ACTV No. 5 orange city buses. Tickets for buses must be bought before boarding from the office inside the arrivals terminal. Buses depart from the concourse outside the terminal. You can also take a water taxi to most points within the city (20 minutes) but the prices are high (over L100,000). A less expensive public water launch makes the trip (50 minutes) to San Marco and the Lido. Tickets are available from an office close to the arrivals terminal exit; the dock is immediately outside.

Arriving by train

- Trains to Venice arrive at Venezia Santa Lucia station, often abbreviated to Venezia SL (☎ 715 555).
- The station is located at the head of the Grand Canal, five minutes' walk from Piazzale Roma, and has frequent *vaporetto* (1, 3, 4, 82) and *motoscafo* (52) boat services to the rest of the city from the quays outside. Be sure the boat is heading in the right direction.
- Note that many through trains stop on the mainland at Mestre station, confusingly called Venezia Mestre (Venezia M), without continuing to Venice proper. Check your train is destined for Santa Lucia; if it is not, catch one of the frequent connecting services at Mestre for the 15-minute trip across the causeway.

Arriving by car

- Cars *must* be left at one of the multi-storey car parks at the Tronchetto (linked by boat 82 to the rest of the city) or the more central Piazzale Roma, from where you can walk or catch boats 1, 3,

4, 52 or 82. Rates start at about L15,000 a day. There are *no* free car parks and no other parking places (cars will be towed away).
• Summer lines on the causeway approaching the city are common. You might consider leaving cars in Mestre and then taking a train (see above).

Customs regulations
• EU nationals do not have to declare goods imported for their personal use.
• Limits for non-EU visitors are: 200 cigarettes or 100 small cigars or 250g of tobacco; 1 liter of spirits (over 22 percent alcohol) or 2 liters of fortified wine (under 22 percent alcohol); 30 milliliters of perfume.

ESSENTIAL FACTS

Tourist information
• **Main tourist office** G13 Palazzetto Selva (white building on the waterfront on the west side of the Giardinetti Reali), Fondamenta delle Farine 522 6356; fax 529 8730 Summer: Mon–Sat 9:10–6:50. Winter: Mon–Sat 9:30–3:30
• **Train station office** D10 529 8711; hotel booking agency 715 016 Daily 8AM–9PM
• **Marco Polo Airport office** 541 5887 Daily. Summer: 9–1, 2–6. Winter: 9:30–3:30
• **Lido office** L16 Gran Viale Santa Maria Elisabetta 6 526 5721 Daily. Summer: 8:30–7:30. Winter: 9:30–3:30

Travel insurance
• A fully comprehensive travel insurance policy is highly recommended.

Opening hours
• **Banks** Mon–Fri 8–1:30 (larger branches also 3–4).

• **Churches** No fixed hours, but generally Mon–Sat 9–12, 3–6; Sun 2–5; except Basilica di San Marco: 9:30–5:30.
• **Museums** Varied, but state-run galleries generally Tue–Sat 9–2, Sun 9–1; city-run and private museums such as the Correr, Palazzo Ducale and Guggenheim usually open all day.
• **Parks** 9–hour before sunset.
• **Post offices** Mon–Sat 8–2, though small offices may not open on Sat, while main offices remain open 8–8 for some services.
• **Restaurants** Many close on Sun evening and all day Mon, plus a statutory closing day once a week (*la chiusura settimanale*).
• **Stores and offices** Generally 9–1, 4–8; most food stores close Wed afternoons except in summer, while other shops close Mon mornings except in summer.

National holidays
• **New Year's Day** January 1
• **Epiphany** January 6
• **Easter Sunday**
• **Easter Monday**
• **Liberation Day** April 25
• **Labor Day** May 1
• **Assumption** August 15
• **All Saints' Day** November 1
• **Immaculate Conception** December 8
• **Christmas Day** December 25
• **Santo Stefano** December 26
• Shops and businesses may also close or observe shorter hours during the Festa della Salute (November 21).
• Good Friday is not a holiday.

Money matters
• The unit of Italian currency is the lira (plural lire), abbreviated to L.
• Currency is issued in the following denominations: (notes) L1,000, L2,000, L5,000, L10,000, L50,000,

and L100,000; and (coins) L5 and L10 (both rare), L50, L100, L200, and L500.

- Note that there are two new small L50 and L100 coins, both still in circulation with the older and larger coins.
- The L200 telephone token (*gettone*) can be used as a coin.
- Foreign-exchange facilities (*cambio*) are available at banks and kiosks throughout the city, but especially around the station, Rialto and San Marco.
- American Express offers competitive exchange rates

  ✚ G12 ✉ Salizzada San Moisè, San Marco 1471
  ☎ Emergency toll-free 1678/72 000
  🕐 Summer: Mon–Sat 8–8. Rest of year: Mon–Fri 9–5:30, Sat 9–12:30.

Women travelers

- Women visiting Venice on their own should have few problems in the city, which is generally extremely safe, but parks and the station area should be avoided late at night.

Places of worship

- **Anglican** St. George's ✚ E13 ✉ Campo San Vio.
- **Catholic (English mass)** San Moisè ✚ G12 ✉ Campo San Moisè, San Marco; and the Basilica di San Marco (English readings Sun at 6) ✚ G/H12 ✉ Piazza San Marco. English-language confessions can be heard on Sun mornings at the Basilica; I Gesuiti ✚ G/H10 ✉ Campo dei Gesuiti; Scalzi ✚ D10 ✉ Fondamenta degli Scalzi; SS Giovanni e Paolo ✚ H11 ✉ Campo SS Giovanni e Paolo; the Redentore ✚ F15 ✉ Campo SS Redentore, Giudecca; and San Giorgio Maggiore ✚ H14 ✉ Isola di San Giorgio Maggiore.
- **Jewish** ✚ E9 ✉ Ghetto Vecchio ☎ 715 012.

Student travelers

- Discounts are available for student travellers in some city museums.

Time differences

- US Eastern Standard Time is six hours behind Italy, and Pacific Standard Time is nine hours behind.
- Italy is one hour ahead of British time, except for a brief period in October when they are the same (note that EU regulations may standardize hour changes).
- Sydney is eight hours ahead of Italy in summer.

Toilets

- Restrooms are located at Piazzale Roma (✚ C11), the train station (✚ C/D10), the west side of the Accademia bridge (✚ E13), off Campo San Bartolomeo (✚ G11), by the Giardinetti Reali (✚ G12/13), on Calle Erizzo near the church of San Martino (✚ J12), and in the Albergo Diurno (Day Hotel) behind the Ala Napoleonica on Ramo Primo a Ascensione (✚ G12).
- In bars and cafés ask for *il gabinetto* or *il bagno*.
- Do not confuse *signori* (men) with *signore* (women).

Electricity

- Current is 220 volts AC (50 cycles), but is suitable for 240-volt appliances.
- Plugs are of the Continental two-round-pin variety.

Etiquette

- Do not wear shorts, miniskirts, or skimpy tops in churches.
- Do not intrude while church services are in progress.
- Do not eat or drink in churches.
- Many churches forbid the use of flashes, or ban photography.
- There are few no-smoking areas in restaurants or public places, but smoking is banned on public transportation (including boats).

PUBLIC TRANSPORTATION

- Venice is a compact city, and the occasions when you need to use its public transportation surprisingly few. But while walking in such a beautiful place is an obvious pleasure, so, too, is the experience of taking a boat.

Public transportation agency

- Venice's public transportation is run by the Azienda del Consorzio Trasporti Veneziano (ACTV), with information offices in Piazzale Roma and Corte dell'Albero, San Marco 3880. Mainland buses and boats: ☎ 528 7886.

Boats

- ACTV runs two basic types of boat: the general-purpose *vaporetto*, and the faster *motoscafo*. Both follow set routes and are numbered—look for the number at the front of the boat. As the same number boat may run in two directions (up and down the Grand Canal, for example), it is vital at the quays—which usually have separate boarding points for each direction—to make sure you board a boat heading in the right direction. This is particularly true at the Ferrovia and San Zaccaria, both busy termini for several routes.
- The web of boat routes around Venice is not as confusing as it first seems. The basic route is Line 1 along the Grand Canal (Piazzale Roma–San Marco–Lido and back). Line 82 also follows the Grand Canal, but has fewer stops; lines 3 and 4 are faster summer-only services. A second 82 boat runs from San Zaccaria to Piazzale Roma by way of the Giudecca. The other boat you may use is Line 12, which runs to the islands of Murano, Burano, and Torcello from the Fondamente Nuove. The ferry information throughout this guide gives the nearest stop as well as the line number.
- Tickets can be bought at most landing stages, on board boats (with a surcharge), and at shops or tobacconists with an ACTV sticker. Tickets are valid only for the route for which they are issued; there is usually a flat fare along the length of the route so the price is the same for one stop or ten stops. Tickets, except those bought individually for Line 1, must be validated in machines at each landing stage before boarding. Heavy spot fines are levied if you are caught traveling without a ticket.
- Three tourist tickets are available: the *Biglietto 24 Ore*, valid on all lines for 24 hours; the *Biglietto 72 Ore*, valid for three days; and the *Biglietto Isole*, valid for travel one way (with stopovers) on Line 12 to Murano, Burano, and Torcello.
- ACTV runs a reduced service throughout the night on most routes. Exact times are posted on timetables at every quay. Tickets can be bought on board.

Water taxis

- Venice's water taxis are fast but extremely expensive. The basic rate is around L35,000 for seven minutes, plus L500 for every additional 15 seconds. Surcharges are levied for each piece of luggage, for trips between 10PM and 7AM, and for each additional passenger over a maximum of four. You can hail a taxi on a canal, but it is usually easier to call by phone—which means around L10,000 on the clock before you start (☎ 523 5775, 522 2303, 716 124, 522 1265 or 523 0575).

Taxis

- For rides to and from the mainland there are taxi stands at Piazzale Roma (☎ 523 7774); Marco Polo Airport (☎ 526 5975); and at the railway station at Mestre (☎ 929 499). Otherwise, call Radio Taxi (☎ 936 222).

Traghetti

- As there are only three bridges across the Grand Canal, Venice's *traghetti* (ferries) provide an invaluable service. Using old gondolas, they ply back and forth at seven strategic points. Quays are usually obscure, so look for the little yellow "Traghetto" signs. Crossings currently cost L600, which you hand to the ferryman as you board. Venetians usually stand, but nobody minds if you sit unless the boat is crowded. Be careful with small children, and watch your balance when the boat pushes off.

MEDIA & COMMUNICATIONS

Telephones

- Telecom Italia (TI) provides public telephones in bars, on the streets and in TI offices. All are indicated by red or yellow signs showing a telephone dial and receiver. Venice has TI booths in Piazzale Roma ✚ C11 🕐 8AM–9:30PM; and the main post office ✚ G11 ✉ Fondaco dei Tedeschi 🕐 8:15–7.

- Phones accept L100, L200, and L500 coins, as well as the L200 *gettone* token. Most also accept phone cards (*schede telefoniche*), available in L5,000, L10,000, and L15,000 denominations from tobacco shops, TI offices, automatic dispensers, or stores displaying a TI sticker. Remember to tear the corner off the card before using it.

- Peak periods are weekdays 8–1, off-peak is 1–8, and calls are cheap at all other times. The cheap international rate covers the weekend and 8PM–8AM during the week.

- The dial tone is alternating long and short pips. A series of rapid pips means you are being connected, while a series of long beeps indicates a ringing telephone at the other end. More rapid beeps means "engaged."

- For international calls, use a phone card or a *telefono a scatti*—a kiosk where you speak first and pay when your call is over (found in some bars, hotels, post offices, and tourist offices, and in most TI offices). Dial 00 for an international line followed by the country code. The code for Italy when calling from abroad is 39.

- To make a collect call, dial 15 (Europe) or 170 (intercontinental) and ask to make *una chiamata con pagamento a destinazione*.

- The area code for Venice is 041 (telephone numbers in this book omit the code).

Post offices

- Venice's central post office (*posta* or *ufficio postale*) is near the Rialto bridge ✚ G11 ✉ Palazzo delle Poste, Fondaco dei Tedeschi ☎ 522 0606 🕐 Mon–Fri 8:15–5:30, Sat 8:15–1.

- Another larger office lies just west of Piazza San Marco ✚ G12 ✉ Calle dell'Ascensione 528 5949 🕐 Mon–Sat 8:15–2.

- Stamps (*francobolli*) are available from post offices, or from tobacco shops (*tabacchi*) displaying a blue "T" sign.

- Mailboxes are small and red and are marked *Poste* or *Lettere*. They usually have two slots—one for local mail (*Città*), the other for destinations further afield (*Altre Destinazione*).

- International mail sent to and from Venice can take up to three weeks to arrive. You can speed things up by sending post *espresso* (express) or *raccomandata* (registered).
- Address poste restante letters Fermo Posta, Fondaco dei Tedeschi, 30100 Venezia. Mail can be collected Mon–Sat 8:15AM– 7PM. Take a passport when collecting mail and be prepared to pay a small fee. Filing can be haphazard, so ask staff to check under both your first and last names.

Telex & telegrams

- These can be sent from Venice's main post office or by calling 186, or 170 for international telegrams.

Newspapers & magazines

- Venice's two main local news-papers are *Il Gazzettino* and *La Nuova Venezia*. Both contain listings for the city.
- Quality national papers include the center-left *La Repubblica* and center-right *Corriere della Sera*.
- *Corriere dello Sport* and the *Gazzetta dello Sport*, two exclu-sively sports-based papers, are also popular.
- News magazines (*riviste*) such as *L'Espresso* and *Panorama* also enjoy a large readership.
- Foreign newspapers are readily available in Venice, usually from late afternoon on the day of issue. Kiosks at the train station are the best source.

Radio & television

- Italian radio and television offer many deregulated national and local stations, including several based in the Veneto region around Venice. Major national tele-vision stations divide between the channels of the state RAI network

(RAI 1, 2, and 3) and the channels founded by Silvio Berlusconi (Canale 5, Rete 4, and Italia Uno).

EMERGENCIES

Crime

- Venice's many tourists are an obvious target for the unscrupu-lous, but by using common sense and taking a few precautions you should stay safe. Report thefts to your hotel and then to the main police station, which has a department to deal with visitors' problems (✉ Questura, Via San Nicolodi 22, Marghera ☎ 271 5511). They will issue you with a document (*una denuncia*) to send in with your insurance claims. Report lost passports to the police and your consulate or embassy.
- For police in an emergency, telephone 112 or 113.
- Carry cash in a belt or pouch, never in a pocket.
- Do not carry large amounts of cash. Use credit cards or traveler's checks.
- Wear your camera and never put it down on café tables. Beware of strap-cutting thieves.
- Do not flaunt valuables. Better still, leave them at home.
- Leave jewelry in the hotel safe (not in rooms), especially items such as chains and earrings which can easily be snatched.
- Hold bags across your front, not just hung over one shoulder where they can be rifled or grabbed.
- Beware of pickpockets on water buses, in markets or wherever groups of tourists gather.
- After dark, avoid noncommercial parts of the city, parks, and the area around the train station.
- Always lock your car, and never leave luggage, cameras, or valuables inside.

Consulates

- **Australia** ✉ Via Alessandria 215, Rome ☎ 06/852 721
- **Austria** ✉ Santa Croce 251 ☎ 524 0556
- **Belgium** ✉ San Marco 1470 ☎ 522 4124
- **Canada** ✉ Via G B Rossi 27, Rome ☎ 06/445 981
- **Denmark** ✉ San Marco 466/G ☎ 520 0822
- **France** ✉ Zattere 1397 ☎ 522 4319
- **Netherlands** ✉ San Marco 423 ☎ 528 3416
- **New Zealand** ✉ Via Zara 28, Rome ☎ 06/440 2928
- **Norway** ✉ Rotonda Garibaldi, Mestre ☎ 534 0447
- **Republic of Ireland** ✉ Piazza Campitelli 3, Rome ☎ 06/697 9121
- **Switzerland** ✉ Zattere, Dorsoduro 810 ☎ 520 3944 or 522 5996
- **UK** ✉ Via San Paolo 7, Milan ☎ 02/723 001
- **USA** ✉ Via Principe Amedeo 2/10, Milan ☎ 02/290 351

Emergency telephone numbers

- Emergency services (police, fire and ambulance) ☎ 113
- **Police** (*Carabinieri*) ☎ 112
- **Questura** (Venice Police Station) ☎ 271 5511
- **Fire** (*Vigili di Fuoco*) ☎ 115
- **Ambulance** ☎ 523 0000
- **Hospital and first aid** (Ospedale Civile) ☎ 529 4517

Lost property

- **City streets** ☎ 270 8225 or 520 8844
- **Buses or boats** ☎ 272 2111 or 272 2179
- **Train or station** ☎ 785 238
- **Airport** ☎ 260 6436
- Report losses of passports to the police and your consulate.
- Report general losses to the main police station ✉ Questura, Via San Nicolodi 22, Marghera ☎ 271 5511.

Health

- Likely hazards include too much

sun, air pollution and biting insects.
- Water is safe to drink unless marked *acqua non potabile*.
- Condoms (*profilatici*) are available over the counter from chemists and most supermarkets.
- Take out health insurance before traveling and keep any receipts for medicine and treatment. Free medical treatment is available to citizens of EU countries, but to be eligible you must take the form E111.
- Pharmacies (*una farmacia*) are identified by a green cross and have the same opening hours as shops, but open late on a rota displayed on pharmacy doors. Staff can give advice on minor ailments and dispense many medicines over the counter, including some only available on prescription in other countries. Remember to bring any prescriptions that might be required to obtain medicine.
- If you wish to see a doctor (*un medico*), enquire at your hotel or call ☎ 531 4481. For first aid (*pronto soccorso*) or hospital treatment, visit the Ospedale Civile ✚ H10/11 ☎ Campo SS Giovanni e Paolo ☎ 529 4517.
- Vaccinations are unnecessary for entry into Italy unless you are travelling from a known infected area. Check current requirements if you are travelling from the Far East, Africa, South America, or the Middle East.

LANGUAGE

- Italians respond well to foreigners who make an effort to speak their language, however badly. Many Italians speak at least some English, and most upscale hotels and restaurants have multilingual staff.
- All Italian words are pronounced

as written, with each vowel and consonant sounded. The letter c is hard, as in English "cat," except when followed by i or e, when it becomes the soft ch of "children." The same applies to g when followed by i or e—soft in *giardino*, as in the English "giant"; hard in *gatto*, as in "gate." Words ending in o are almost always masculine in gender (plural ending—i); those ending in a are feminine (plural ending—e)

- Use the polite, third person (*lei*) to speak to strangers and the second person (*tu*) to friends or children

Courtesies

good morning buon giorno
good afternoon/good evening buona sera
good night buona notte
hello/goodbye (informal) ciao
hello (answering the telephone) pronto
goodbye arrivederci
please per favore
thank you (very much) (mille) grazie
you're welcome prego
how are you? (polite/informal) come sta/stai?
I'm fine sto bene
I'm sorry mi dispiace
excuse me/I beg your pardon mi scusi
excuse me (in a crowd) permesso

Basic vocabulary

yes sì
no no
I do not understand no ho capito
left/right sinistra/destra
entrance entrata
exit uscita
open/closed aperto/chiuso
upstairs sopra
downstairs da basso
inside dentro
come in! avanti!

good/bad buono/cattivo
big/small grande/piccolo
with con
without senza
more più
less meno
near vicino
far lontano
hot/cold caldo/freddo
early presto
late ritardo
here qui
there là
now adesso
later più tardi
today oggi
tomorrow domani
yesterday ieri
morning mattino
afternoon pommeriggio
how much is it? quant'è?
expensive caro
inexpensive a buon mercato
when? quando?
do you have …? avete …?

Emergencies

help! aiuto!
where is the nearest telephone? dov'è il telefono più vicino?
there has been an accident c'è stato un incidente
call the police chiamate la polizia
call a doctor/an ambulance chiamate un medico/un'ambulanza
first aid pronto soccorso
where is the nearest hospital? dov'è l'ospedale più vicino?

Numbers

one uno, una
two due
three tre
four quattro
five cinque
six sei
seven sette
eight otto
nine nove
ten dieci

93

INDEX

CityPack
Venice

Published in the United States by Fodor's Travel Publications, Inc.
Published in the United Kingdom by AA Publishing

Fodor's is a registered trademark of Fodor's Travel Publications, Inc.

ISBN 0- 679-03429-3
First Edition

FODOR'S CITYPACK VENICE

AUTHOR *Tim Jepson*
CARTOGRAPHY *The Automobile Association*
RV Reise- und Verkehrsverlag
COVER DESIGN *Tigist Getachew, Fabrizio La Rocca*

COPY EDITOR *Susi Bailey*
VERIFIER *Tom Bruce-Gardyne*
AMERICANIZER *Sean Connolly*
INDEXER *Marie Lorimer*

Acknowledgments

The Automobile Association wishes to thank the following photographers and libraries for their assistance in the preparation of this book:
The Bridgeman Art Library Ltd, London 31a Supper at the House of th Levi, 1573 by Veronese, (Paolo Caliari), Gallerie dell'Accademia, Venice, 50 The Miracle of the Cross on San Lorenzo Bridge, 1500 by Gentile Bellini, Gallerie dell'Accademia, Venice, 51b
St. George Killing the Dragon by Carpaccio, Vittore, Scuola di San Giorgio degli Schiavoni, Venice; Mary Evans Picture Library 12a, 12b, 12c; John Hesteltine Archive 42; Spectrum Colour Library 24b.
The remaining photographs are held in the Association's own photo library (AA PHOTO LIBRARY) and were taken by Dario Miterdieri, pages 5a, 8, 16, 18, 20b, 21, 27b, 28, 29a, 30a, 30b, 33a, 35a, 37a, 37b, 39a, 43a, 43b, 45, 46, 49b, 51a, 53, 54, 55b, 57, 58, 59; Richard Newton, pages 23a, 32b, 52a; Clive Sawyer, pages 1, 5b, 6/7, 13a, 13b, 15, 17, 19, 23b, 24a, 25, 26, 27a, 29b, 33b, 34a, 34b, 33b, 34a, 34b, 35b, 36, 38a, 38b, 39b, 40a, 41a, 41b, 44a, 44b, 47b, 48a, 48b, 49a, 52b, 55a, 56, 60, 63a, 63b, 87a, 87b and Rosie Walford, pages 32a and 47a.

Special sales

Fodor's Travel Publications are available at special discounts for bulk purchases (100 copies or more) for sales promotions or premiums. Special editions, including personalized covers, excerpts of existing guides, and corporate imprints, can be created in large quantities for special needs. For more information write to Special Marketing, Fodor's Travel Publications, 201 East 50th St., New York NY 10022.

Color separation by Daylight Colour Art Pte Ltd, Singapore

Manufactured by Dai Nippon Printing Co. (Hong Kong) Ltd

10 9 8 7 6 5 4 3 2

Titles in the Citypack series